DATE DUE

MR 6 '95			
JE 10 '09			

Demco, Inc. 38 293

Toward Independence:
The Baltic Popular Movements

Published in cooperation
with Radio Free Europe/Radio Liberty, Inc.

Toward Independence:
The Baltic Popular Movements

EDITED BY
Jan Arveds Trapans

Westview Press
BOULDER, SAN FRANCISCO, & OXFORD

Published in 1991 in the United States of America by Westview Press, Inc., 5500 Central Avenue, Boulder, Colorado 80301, and in the United Kingdom by Westview Press, 36 Lonsdale Road, Summertown, Oxford OX2 7EW

Library of Congress Cataloging-in-Publication Data
Toward independence : the Baltic popular movements / edited by Jan
   Arveds Trapans.
      p. cm.
   ISBN 0-8133-8144-4
   1. Baltic States—History—Autonomy and independence movements.
2. Nationalism—Baltic States.   I. Trapans, Jan Arveds.
DK502.7.T68   1991
947′.4—dc20   90-23124
                                                                                CIP

Printed and bound in the United States of America

The paper used in this publication meets the requirements
of the American National Standard for Permanence of Paper
for Printed Library Materials Z39.48-1984.

10   9   8   7   6   5   4   3   2

Contents

Preface

As this study goes to press, political developments in the Baltic states continue to move toward independence. These developments are guided by the three popular movements and are proceeding along the analytic lines drawn by the Baltic and Soviet experts represented in this book. The movements, having declared for independence, have also gained an upper hand in the parliaments. Communist parties and elements of the old system continue to fight a tenacious and not entirely unsuccessful rear-guard battle for survival and influence. Baltic declarations for independence are emulated in one Soviet republic after another, including the Russian Republic led by Boris Yeltsin. The Western press seeks to assess and interpret all of this, while Western political leaders search for a coherent and consistent "Baltic policy."

This publication arises from a conference convoked by Radio Free Europe/Radio Liberty, Inc., in September 1989. As principal broadcasters to the Baltic states and close observers of the momentous events unfolding in them, we believed the time was right for assembling leaders of the popular movements, Western scholars and journalists, and our own analysts and broadcasting staff for a discussion of what had occurred and what was likely to occur in the drive toward independence. *Toward Independence: The Baltic Popular Movements* is but one result of the conference.

We hope the various opinions expressed in this volume will provide Western readers with insights into the profound changes now taking place in the Baltic—changes that have significance not only for the Baltic states themselves but for the entire Soviet Union.

E. Eugene Pell, President
Radio Free Europe/Radio Liberty, Inc.

PART ONE

Introduction

1

Introduction

Jan Arveds Trapans

In a few short years, the Soviet Union has changed beyond recognition. The Baltic popular movements stand at the forefront of this change, serving as inspirations and models for similar movements in other parts of the Soviet Union. The demand for the rights of nations is no longer unique to the Estonian, Latvian and Lithuanian movements. Moscow's policy of centralization and russification is equally resented by other nations in the Soviet empire. Demands the Balts made in 1988 have been repeated six months or a year later by others. For instance, the Balts' demand for "republican sovereignty," meaning broad economic and political autonomy, has been picked up by all other movements. With many similar issues, the Baltic model is unmistakable. Opponents of change have spoken of a "Baltic disease" infecting the political body of the Soviet Union. The Baltic Popular Fronts have formulated demands that, if successful, will change the fate not only of the Baltic states themselves but of the entire Soviet empire.

But Gorbachev must be given his due. Without his great shift away from Brezhnev's stagnation to reform, the Baltic movements would not have traveled as far and as fast as they have; probably, they would have been ruthlessly driven underground. With *glasnost* and *perestroika*, the Baltic movements emerged, fed from their own sources and governed by their own dynamics. By late 1988 or early 1989, Baltic aims and Moscow's hopes, Popular Fronts and *perestroika*, had definitely parted ways. If Gorbachev set the stage and drew the curtain for the action to begin, the Balts wrote much of the play and assigned most of the roles themselves.

Gorbachev has said that the Soviet Union is to be remade into a broad confederation. Moscow will redraw the distribution of power between the center and the republics and reshape relations among nationalities. This restructuring was not a part of Gorbachev's *perestroika* when he first undertook to reform the Soviet Union. It was forced upon him by the national demands first formulated by the Balts, demands he never anticipated. He claims that the present Soviet state will be remade according to old but still valid Leninist nationality principles. But the Balts themselves say they want nothing to do with new federations or old Leninist principles. Their sole interest at present is in regaining their independence and rejoining the West.

It is one thing, however, to demand or declare political independence. It is another matter to disentangle the Baltic economy from the centralizing clutches of Moscow, to rid agriculture of the inefficient collective farms and to replace Soviet bureaucrats with efficient businessmen and managers. Ultimately, Gorbachev may be able to let down the curtain on the Baltic drama. Though he may not be able to decide when and how the play will end, he still has the ability to interrupt and delay a certain act for a long time.

Independence is the strongest argument the Baltic movements have. Summarized, their claims are as follows. All three Baltic states were independent from 1918 to 1940. All three enjoyed prosperity. All three were part of Western Europe with a living standard not far behind that of the Scandinavian countries. For years, the Communist Party has insisted repeatedly, even desperately, that in 1940 a "socialist revolution," spearheaded by Communists, took place in the Baltic, leading all three nations to join the Soviet Union voluntarily. Today, historians—Party historians included—will admit that Baltic independence was lost in August, 1939, when Molotov and Ribbentrop signed the Nazi-Soviet Pact accompanied by a secret protocol that gave the Baltic states to Moscow. There was no desire by the Baltic nations to join the Soviet Union in 1940: the decision was made by Hitler in an offer to Stalin. There was no "socialist revolution" in 1940 but a military occupation of three independent countries by the Red Army. The role of the local Communists, numbering only a few hundred, was that of traitors and quislings.

The facts about the seizure of the Baltic states have been known to Western historians for years. Nowadays, the same facts are read repeatedly by Baltic audiences, even in newspapers controlled by the Party. Evidence drawn from history is providing arguments for contemporary politics. When Gorbachev states that he wants to construct a new confederation built on true Leninist principles, the Baltic movements answer that new federations or old principles are of little concern to them. They never joined any confederation to begin with. The Red Army came in illegally in 1940. The time has come for it to get out. Thereupon the Baltic states, which have been under military occupation for 50 years, will be able to exercise the full rights belonging to independent republics.

The Communist parties of the Baltic states are in a difficult position. Their utter inability to deal with the situation is evident to all. First, the Baltic Communist organizations were to inaugurate *perestroika*: they did nothing. Second, they were to convert the incipient popular movements into helpful allies of *perestroika*: they failed. Third, they faced the popular movements in elections: they were demolished. Losing power, scrambling to retain what they could of privilege and position, internally divided, the Baltic parties fell away from Moscow and, in the fall, broke into fragments. This cleavage has followed nationality lines. The Russian Party members tend to remain loyal to Moscow (though they are not loyal to Gorbachev); the Baltic members profess loyalty to their nations. *Perestroika* has few loyalists.

The Baltic Popular Fronts are large. They have members or supporters numbering in the hundreds of thousands; they have organized demonstrations where as many as a million people, perhaps more, participate. The total number of Estonians, Latvians and Lithuanians, it should be recalled, is only some five million. The sheer size of the movements has overwhelmed and overawed the Communists. In 1990, they are the most potent political force in the Baltic. We read about the Baltic Popular Fronts as revolutionary and single-minded movements. Revolutionary they are. Their aim today is definite: independence. But they emerged in a tumultuous fashion and have not been as cohesive and single-minded in their period of emergence as accounts found in the West sometimes imply.

This is true in any revolutionary situation. Events in the Baltic have provided us with a nonviolent revolution that aims to change utterly the politics, economics, state structure and intellectual world of the *ancien régime*. Part Two of this volume provides three views of how the movements developed: first, an account of the sweep of events in Lithuania, where a political interplay and conflict between Lithuania's Popular Front, Sajudis, and the Communist Party shifted and accelerated the politics of the national revolution; second, a study of the emergence and internal dynamics of Latvia's popular movement, which arose from both radical and moderate sources that have contested each other's control over the direction and policies of the movement; and third, a presentation in which leaders of Estonian, Latvian and Ukrainian movements relate their views on the present political situation, estimate what the future may hold and indicate political moves that may be required. Although these chapters provide a fragmentary picture of the Baltic movements, they also give a sense of the rush and conflict in which the popular movements took shape.

The other picture, the tenacious resistance in the Soviet Union to centrifugal forces, is described in Part Three. Three counterforces, distinct in nature but related in purpose, are acting in concert to maintain the *ancien régime* in the Baltic. First, there is the Communist Party—troubled, fragmented, but still visibly present on the political stage, quietly guarding its power behind the scenes. Although it is losing its overt power and ideological purpose, much of its hidden strength remains in the nomenklatura. Second, there are the recent migrants to the Baltic region, mostly though not exclusively Russian—surprised, confused and antagonized by an unexpected and strong drive for Baltic independence. As Popular Fronts arose in the Baltic, so did "interfronts" (short for "international fronts"), which purport to defend the rights of these recent immigrants. And, third, there are the larger, more impersonal, forces, less visible to the Western observer: the economic machinery of centralized and bureaucratic socialism, deliberately constructed by Moscow over the years to hold the Baltic within the Soviet Union. Reforming or altering the centralized economic structure, which binds the Baltic republics almost as firmly today as three years ago, when the popular movements first broke loose, will be a difficult and long task. Baltic economists themselves agree that while they know where they want to move they do not quite know how they are going to go about it. A Baltic economic planner reminds one very much of a man standing on the eastern bank of a stream showing with broad gestures his intent to leap over to the western one: but the stream is broad and the eastern bank is soggy and uncertain underfoot. One leap will not do it. Stepping-stones must be placed in the stream. Less picturesquely, there probably will be stages of economic reform; the Balts will have to reform themselves away from Moscow—from a Stalinist command economy to an East European variety of socialist market economy—until they can make a final leap into a market economy.

The complex issue of economic reform contains all the submerged forces pulling the Baltic back into a slowly circling Moscow vortex. Here we find Communists, no longer parts of a cohesive, obedient Party structure responsive to Moscow's commands, but still holding responsible positions in economic administration, linked by past careers and a mutual need to survive in new and threatening circumstances. Here we find Russian administrators, also holding responsible positions in enterprise and the bureaucracy, bent on maintaining Moscow's central power as much as possible. And here we find a mass of Russian-speaking immigrants, most frequently employed in factories, who, in their fear about the revolutionary political developments around them, provide rank and file for those who resist any and all change. The reaction, smallest in numbers in Lithuania, largest in Latvia, has a leadership well placed in positions to delay and frustrate economic and political moves away from "the center."

For all that, the center is under severe attack from all sides. The Baltic challenge to Moscow was soon followed by others: in Armenia, Belorussia, Ukraine, Moldavia and Georgia. Among the first to feel Baltic influences were the two republics that are closest geographically: Belorussia and

Ukraine. In Part Four, the similarities and the direct ties between the Baltic movements and those of their immediate neighbors are explored. Here we definitely find a clear situation where Baltic national demands provided examples and inspiration for other movements. Furthermore, people from the Baltic movements deliberately helped the other republics to organize, though it would be inaccurate to say that the Balts conspired to bring unrest to neighboring republics (such charges have been heard from defenders of the Brezhnevite system). In their demand for national rights, the Baltic movements extended a challenge to the empire that strikes at the heart of the Marxist-Leninist principles upon which the Soviet Union is built.

No less of a challenge has been extended to the Western community of experts on the Soviet Union. A few years ago, it was generally accepted that the Soviet Union, as shaped by successive Party leaders, would lumber, inertia laden, into the next century. Forecasts told that of all the problems that would trouble the Soviet empire (scholars did agree that problems were in store for Moscow), the "nationality issue" would be the smallest; most frequently, in fact, the nationality question was not mentioned at all. Therefore, many Western experts now must review their own analytical principles as well as the salient facts about the Soviet Union. A probing essay in Part Four asks whether an end of the Soviet empire does not demand a reexamination of Western illusions about it.

Most of what has taken place in the Baltic has taken place under the full light of publicity. When Latvia's Popular Front held its founding congress in Riga, detailed information on its proceedings could be read in newspapers available in small American towns. The West is interested in the Baltic. As is noted in the discussion in Part Five, what the Western press writes about the Baltic really matters, since its reports affect Western perceptions of Baltic aspirations, of Baltic history and Baltic peoples, and, ultimately, they affect the attitude of Western governments. In the long term, Western perceptions will come to bear on the fate of the Baltic peoples.

One advantage the Baltic nations possess that others in the Soviet empire do not is a large community in the West. At the end of World War II, large parts of the Baltic populations left their countries and fled westward: they had lived under the Stalinist regime from 1940 to 1941 and knew what it would bring. For half a century, the Baltic émigré community has survived, decreasing in numbers but well coordinated and politically potent (as US congressmen know), with a second generation of professionals, businessmen and academics. For years, the Communist Party attacked the émigré community and simultaneously attempted to neutralize it by insinuating propaganda into its midst. But, almost overnight, the role of the émigré community has altered. As is described in the last chapter of this book, it has changed from a dangerous enemy to a potentially strong ally. Emigré political groups in Western capitals now are asked to represent the cause of the popular movements. Professionals are asked to be expert advisers, and academics are asked to restore Western-style education in Baltic universities. Even Communist Party members have written of the good Western businessmen might bring to restoring Baltic economies. The picture of the emigration in Baltic publications today is one of a wise member of the family who knows best how to build a bridge over which the others will walk to the West.

The role the West can play in aiding the Baltic nations today is described most specifically by Marju Lauristin, one of the leaders of Estonia's Popular Front, in her essay in Part Five. Her look toward the West encompasses a view of the past, of what the Baltic was before the sovietization and of how the damage can be reversed. She looks at the role of Western governments and press, and the potential of the émigré community. Finally, she comes to grips with what the Balts and the West may have misunderstood about each other.

PART TWO

The Movements

2

Sajudis: National Revolution in Lithuania

V. Stanley Vardys

The complex political, economic and social changes now taking place in Lithuania can best be described as part of a broad-based movement toward national independence and democracy. Lietuvos Persitvarkymos Sajudis (Lithuania's *Perestroika* Movement), which is the main engine of this drive toward self-determination and self-government, has made three separate declarations: a declaration of moral independence in November, 1988, a declaration of spiritual independence in February, 1989, and, in May of 1989, what is, in fact, no less than a declaration of political independence.[1] It has quickly won grass-roots support among almost all segments of Lithuanian society. "We are convinced," declared the three Baltic Popular Fronts in May, 1989, "that alongside the process of broadening openness, mass democratic movements are the only guarantee for the continuation and irreversibility of the radical restructuring of society."[2]

The emergence of Sajudis was initially made possible by Mikhail Gorbachev's *glasnost* and *perestroika*. Gorbachev's new approach was to be a tool that would subject the Soviet Union's bureaucrats to a degree of popular control and promote initiative from outside the regime. In Lithuania, something entirely different from what the General Secretary intended has taken place. The Lithuanians have used Gorbachev's original arguments and rationale for *glasnost* and *perestroika* to give their own aims

---

[1] The substance of the three declarations was published in *Atgimimas* (the official publication of Sajudis) on November 22, 1988, and February 17, 1988, and in *Tiesa*, May 19, 1989.

[2] "Appeal to the Democratic Movements of the Soviet Union," The Baltic Council, May 14, 1989. A telefax copy of the statement was secured by the Lithuanian Information Center, Brooklyn, New York.

legitimacy, while those aims have gone far beyond his. Gorbachev seeks "pluralistic socialism"; the Lithuanians seek a pluralistic society. In restructuring the economy, Gorbachev intended to introduce a degree of reform; Sajudis, like the other Baltic popular movements, has made radical demands concerning private ownership and management. Finally, the question of political change is proceeding in a very charged atmosphere of Lithuanian national consciousness. Though, as Western observers have argued, Gorbachev may have attempted to direct the energies of popular movements such as Sajudis into supporting his own designs, he also may have awakened the tiger of national self-determination. It is now an open question whether the Communist Party will be able to ride this tiger to reform and its own safety or not.

Glasnost came to Lithuania later than to the other two Baltic republics because of the conservatism of the Lithuanian Communist Party and the cautious nature of the Lithuanians in general. After the death of First Secretary Antanas Snieckus, who had held office until 1976, the Party leadership was inherited by mediocre representatives of the apparat. Snieckus's successor Petras Griskevicius talked of *perestroika* as a revolutionary process, but he had a very narrow interpretation of *glasnost*. The past could be reexamined, he conceded, but all historical events had to be judged from the perspective of class position and public criticism was permissible only if it did not obstruct harmonious collective efforts.[3]

Griskevicius died on November 14, 1987, but his successor as First Secretary, Ringaudas Songaila, followed the same course. The Lithuanian Communist Party plenum, on January 26, 1988, complained that the Party had not dealt strongly enough with "alien philosophies" and stated that "international" and "class-conscious" education had to be emphasized and "nationalist and clerical extremists" strongly rebuffed.[4]

Like the Party, the intellectual and professional class in Lithuania was cautious about reforms. There are several reasons for this outlook. In Lithuania, Soviet rule has been less threatening than it has in Latvia and Estonia, where masses of immigrants have been brought in, sharply reducing the native population. The proportion of Lithuanians has remained at a steady 80 percent and the proportion of Russian immigrants under ten percent, as in the 1960s and 1970s. The Lithuanians' caution was also prompted by skepticism. Doubting the longevity of Gorbachev's rule and disillusioned because of previous experience with reform efforts, most Lithuanians were reluctant to take the initiative.

---

[3] Griskevicius outlined his themes on *perestroika* in "The Focus of *Perestroika* is Man," *Pergale* (February, 1987), 3–11 *passim*.

[4] *Sajudzio Zinios* (No. 2, 1988); *Tiesa*, January 29, 1988.

In this general atmosphere of caution, Sajudis came into being on May 23, 1988, at the Lithuanian Academy of Sciences, which established a commission to propose changes in Lithuania's constitution to accommodate democratization, *perestroika* and *glasnost*.[5] Two events solidified the determination by Party and non-Party intellectuals to form a popular movement: the selection of delegates to the 19th Conference of the Communist Party of the Soviet Union (CPSU) and decisions made in Moscow on expanding Lithuania's chemical industry. The delegates to the conference were appointed from above by the Party leadership—in the traditional fashion—and Moscow's decision on the chemical plants ignored the Lithuanian government's decision forbidding further expansion in cities that already were strangling from pollution.[6] On June 3, intellectuals and professionals met to discuss a course of action and an "initiative group" was elected to organize a movement for the support of *perestroika*.

Although Sajudis was rumored to be hostile to the Communist Party leadership, it was not organized against the leadership's wishes. In fact, the new group was not inimical to the Party but simply wished to be independent from it.[7] Many distinguished intellectuals and professionals who were also Party members joined the movement. On the one hand, this indicated a Party split and weakened the ruling organization. On the other hand, Party members within the movement afforded some control and influence and encouraged the building of a consensus.

Sajudis gathered strength in the summer of 1988, using mass meetings, demonstrations and public events to mobilize support and establish its base. Meetings were held to discuss justice to Stalinist and other political victims; the definition of "sovereignty"; the Molotov-Ribbentrop Pact of 1939, in which the Soviets and the Nazis partitioned the Baltic; economic independence; the status of the Lithuanian language; and the release of political prisoners. These public meetings became places in which the anger that had accumulated over decades of Soviet oppression was given free expression. Functioning as an "informal" organization, Sajudis was quickly granted legitimacy by the Lithuanian people.[8]

On June 24, Sajudis called for a "send-off" meeting (attended by 50,000 people) for Party delegates going to the 19th CPSU Conference and on July 9, for a "reception" (attended by 100,000 people) when the delegates returned from Moscow. Speakers at the June 24 meeting asked that the

---

[5] *Tiesa*, January 29, 1988, 2.

[6] *Ibid*. See Saulius Girnius, "The Lithuanian Restructuring Movement," *Radio Free Europe Research*, August 4, 1988.

[7] *Sajudzio Zinios* (No. 2, 1988), 2; *Gimtasis Krastas*, June 9–15, 1988, 3.

[8] Kestutis Girnius, "Three Months of Change in Lithuania," *Radio Free Europe Research*, August 31, 1988.

Party ensure true Soviet or government rule, presumably according to the ideals professed in the October Revolution; restore republican sovereignty according to the correct Leninist concept of the nature of the Soviet Union; bring democracy to Party and government; establish republican citizenship and regulate immigration; and provide opportunities for direct relationships between Lithuania and foreign countries.[9] On August 23, a mass demonstration marking the Molotov-Ribbentrop Pact, attended by an estimated 250,000 people, denounced Stalinism and demanded publication of the secret protocols of the pact, the opening of archives, the rewriting of school history texts and the restoration of republican sovereignty.[10]

The meetings show a political reorientation. On June 24, requests for autonomy were modestly stated, but on August 23, the discussion of the Molotov-Ribbentrop Pact brought the issue of national self-determination to the forefront. Sajudis had changed its priorities. Reform, as required and defined by the Lithuanians, advanced. *Perestroika*, as defined by Moscow, receded.

In an atmosphere of *glasnost* and reform, the Lithuanian Communist Party could not ignore Sajudis's growing power. The two struggled for influence, though their struggle differed from competitions for power in Western systems. Two factors account for this difference. First, Sajudis had broad allegiance from the people and could rely on private donations, but the Party controlled the media and law-enforcement agencies and had considerable financial resources. Second, Sajudis and the Party, by themselves, could not decide the outcome of their contest. This decision only could be made by Moscow.

The Lithuanian Communist Party failed to understand or accept much about Sajudis or about reforms in general. Nevertheless, First Secretary Songaila attempted to march in step with Gorbachev's drum. The government began to study models for future economic self-management and to make plans to revise the republic's constitution to include these changes. At the 19th Party Conference, Songaila made some concessions on cultural questions. Nonetheless, he demanded greater Party influence over Lithuania's informal groups, stressing that only efforts that strengthened and rejuvenated socialism were acceptable and complaining that there was too much *glasnost*. Party bureaucrats sharply criticized Sajudis for not rejecting "nationalists": the Party had fought Lithuanian nationalism for 50 years and could not comprehend that autonomy and reform coming from below had to be undergirded by nationalism.

---

[9] Text in *Gimtasis Krastas*, June 16–22, 1988, 3.

[10] Described in Saulius Girnius, "Massive Demonstration in Lithuania," *Radio Free Europe Research*, August 26, 1988, and *Atgimimas*, September 16, 1988, 15.

Aleksandr Yakovlev, Gorbachev's closest ally in the Politburo, was sent to Lithuania (and to Latvia, where the same difficulties were found) to sort out matters. He urged the Party leadership to avoid confrontation, get involved in directing changes and harness the "national factor" to reforms.[11] The Party made moves in this direction. Russification of education was reversed. Construction of the controversial Ignalina nuclear plant was halted—an unprecedented act of defiance toward Moscow ministries.[12] Yet on September 14, the Party Bureau attacked Sajudis, complaining that it cooperated with people who "openly propagated extremist sentiments" and that some Sajudis followers were in contact with "Western radio [representatives] and with the reactionary part of Lithuanian emigration."[13]

First Secretary Songaila and Second Secretary Nikolai Mikitin were chiefly concerned with defending Party prerogatives in the face of Sajudis's growing power. This attitude eventually would backfire and end their Party careers. On September 28, an overtly nationalist independent organization called the Lithuanian Freedom League organized a meeting in Vilnius to mark the anniversary of the date in 1939 when Hitler agreed that Lithuania should be within the Soviet sphere of influence. The meeting was not sanctioned by the city's administration but was held nonetheless; it was met by violent police attacks, and numbers of demonstrators were injured or arrested.[14] After a summer of peaceful gatherings, the police violence came as a shock to the Lithuanian public. There was mounting criticism against the First Secretary—certainly, police could not have been sent against the demonstrators without his approval—and a few days before the founding congress of Sajudis on October 22, he was replaced by Algirdas Brazauskas. Second Secretary Mikitin was eased out somewhat later and replaced by a Lithuanian-born Russian, Vladimir Berezov, who later would publicly claim he would not be "Moscow's Gauleiter" in Lithuania.[15]

After the fall of Songaila, Sajudis and the Party entered a brief period of amicable relations. Speaking at Sajudis's founding congress, the new First Secretary, Brazauskas, revealed that three days previously he had met

---

[11] Secretary Nikolai Mikitin in *Tiesa*, August 23, 1988. For Yakovlev's visit to Riga, see Dzintra Bungs, "Yakovlev in Latvia: An Exercise in 'Socialist Pluralism,'" *Radio Free Europe Research*, August 26, 1988.

[12] On this issue, see Saulius Girnius, "Continued Controversy over Ignalina Atomic Power Plant," *Radio Free Europe Research*, August 4, 1988, and Saulius Girnius, "Construction Suspended at Ignalina's Atomic Power Plant," *Radio Free Europe Research*, September 3, 1988.

[13] *Tiesa*, September 14, 1988.

[14] Saulius Girnius, "Police Disperse Demonstration," *Radio Free Europe Research*, October 5, 1988.

[15] *Tiesa*, October 23, 1988.

Gorbachev, who sent his greetings to the Lithuanian people and stated that Sajudis was a positive factor in *perestroika*.[16] At the congress, Sajudis agreed that its goals were within the policy of *perestroika*. It would seek sovereignty in all aspects of Lithuania's life, but this sovereignty would be executed within a Leninist Soviet federation. Within six weeks, however, the good relations between the Party and Sajudis had broken down completely, not the least because of Gorbachev's actions. A controversy arose over economics, politics and constitutional issues— over "economic models," "republican sovereignty" and constitutional changes. These complex and interrelated matters carried significance for all three Baltic republics.

In the area of economics, Estonia's Popular Front had worked out a model for reform that subsequently was considered and accepted by a group of Baltic experts in Riga, Latvia, in September, 1988. It was then generally referred to as the Baltic Model.[17] Among its key points were demands that economic reforms should be based upon market principles, that Baltic economic activities must be under the control of their governments, that all natural resources would belong to the republics and that within the All-Union budget the Baltic republics must be distinct entities that levy their own taxes. On November 17, Estonia's Supreme Soviet made a declaration of "republican sovereignty" confirming these demands by placing the republic's legislation above All-Union laws and the All-Union Supreme Soviet. The other two Baltic republics were expected to follow suit.

Earlier, Sajudis's congress had accepted the Baltic economic plan and it had become a part of the movement's platform—acceptable also, or so it appeared, to the Party. All the economic provisions and the changes in political, social and cultural spheres engendered by *perestroika* had to be given a legal framework, and a new draft constitution for Lithuania was prepared under the auspices of the Lithuanian Academy of Sciences early in November. A second draft was approved by Sajudis's council on November 13, and constitutional amendments, republican sovereignty and economic innovations were to be accepted by Lithuania's Supreme Soviet on November 18.

Moscow, however, found the Baltic economic proposals entirely unacceptable. In November, Gorbachev made his own amendments to the All-Union Constitution and outlined provisions for a new Congress of People's Deputies and a new Supreme Soviet. In his scheme, the sovereign

---

[16]   *Ibid.*, October 21, 1988.

[17]   *Atgimimas*, October 10, 1988; *Tiesa*, October 5, 1988. The basic proposals were worked out earlier by Baltic economists. See Saulius Girnius, "Lithuanian and Estonian Economists Jointly Discuss Proposals for Autonomy," *Radio Free Europe Research*, July 13, 1988.

rights of the republics would be restricted and their representation in the new central bodies reduced. Gorbachev's moves and Sajudis's hopes were at cross-purposes.

On November 8, representatives of the three Baltic popular movements met in Riga. There they issued a joint statement opposing Gorbachev's proposals, asking that economic autonomy be legally guaranteed and appealing to the Baltic populations to sign mass petitions supporting their stand.[18] In Lithuania, 1.8 million people would sign the petitions.[19] Sajudis and Moscow were heading toward a collision, with the Lithuanian Communist Party uneasily between them.

On November 17, when Estonia's Supreme Soviet declared republican sovereignty, the political crisis came to a head.[20] Lithuania's First Secretary Brazauskas was immediately called to Moscow. On November 18, Lithuania's Supreme Soviet refused to pass a similar declaration of sovereignty and circumvented the issue of revising the constitution.[21] The decision ruptured the consensus between Sajudis and the Party. Sajudis representatives were incensed, and a crowd outside the Supreme Soviet building, happily waiting for a positive declaration, was infuriated. On November 19, Brazauskas addressed the nation on television in a complex and apologetic speech pleading that the road to sovereignty was extremely complicated and enormously long. Sajudis was not appeased by this speech nor by subsequent Party gestures toward the Catholic church or by its moves to restore patriotic Lithuanian traditions. On November 20, Sajudis issued a declaration of "moral independence" that stated that "Lithuania's will is its highest law . . . only those laws will be respected in Lithuania that do not restrict Lithuania's independence."[22] Sajudis was now in clear opposition and prepared to contest the Communist Party in the elections to the Congress of People's Deputies in the spring of 1989.

Sajudis candidates were first nominated in all electoral districts, but then the two candidates campaigning against Party leaders Brazauskas and Berezov were withdrawn. Sajudis had a positive view of these two men for their personal qualities, leadership abilities and political views.

The Party platform and Sajudis's electoral demands overlapped to a certain extent. The Party expressed support for *perestroika*, promoted the plan for economic autonomy and advocated pluralism of opinions, democracy and *glasnost*, defined as respect for the common values of mankind. Sajudis advocated private farming, on which the Party hedged, and that

---

[18] *Atgimimas*, November 11, 1988, 5.

[19] *Literatura ir menas*, June 17, 1988, 2.

[20] *Tiesa*, October 22, 1988.

[21] *Atgimimas*, November 22, 1988, 3.

[22] *Ibid.*, 5.

military service should be performed in national units stationed within the republic's territory. Both platforms supported Lithuania's sovereignty, but differed greatly on its interpretation. To the Party, sovereignty was still related to the concept of a Leninist Soviet federation. To Sajudis, sovereignty meant "the natural and inalienable right to establish an independent Lithuania." Sajudis further demanded that all other Soviet republics and the Russian Republic (RSFSR) respect the Treaty of 1920 signed by RSFSR and Lithuania recognizing Lithuania as an independent state, and that Moscow publish and declare null and void the Nazi-Soviet agreements of 1939 and 1940 that opened the way "for the occupation and annexation of the Lithuanian Republic."[23] On February 16, 1989, Sajudis's council issued a declaration of "spiritual independence" stating that Lithuania had been annexed by conspiracy and force, and that "international recognition of Lithuanian independence was still valid."[24]

In response, First Secretary Brazauskas claimed Sajudis had changed since June, 1988, and now was pushing Lithuania into ruin. At the Central Committee plenum of February 21, later known as the "black plenum," he said that laws should be passed against violators of rules concerning meetings and demonstrations. But the Party had lost control over the media, the younger generation, the professionals and even over its own membership. The election results were disastrous for the Communists. Sajudis candidates won in 36 of 42 electoral districts, and since Brazauskas and Berezov had run unopposed, the Party could claim only four victories.[25]

After the election, both Sajudis and the Communist Party moved toward establishing a consensus. In Moscow, the members of Sajudis who had been elected to the Congress of Peoples' Deputies met Anatoly Lukyanov, Gorbachev's expert on Lithuanian affairs. Lukyanov urged the Lithuanians to devote themselves to economic affairs, along the lines proposed by Moscow, and asked whether the Lithuanians would recognize the Party's "leading role."[26] From their viewpoint, the Lithuanian deputies attempted to convince Lukyanov that Moscow's plans for economic management could not improve Lithuania's economy. A change in Moscow's attitude can be documented shortly afterwards. On April 21, 1989, *Tiesa*, the Lithuanian Communist Party's official daily, announced that Moscow had admitted the existence of secret protocols signed by the Nazis and the

[23] Saulius Girnius, "The Elections for the USSR Congress of People's Deputies," *Radio Free Europe Research*, March 16, 1989.

[24] *Atgimimas*, February 17, 1989, 1.

[25] Election results were published in *Tiesa*, March 29 and April 11, 1989. See also Saulius Girnius, "Sajudis Candidates Sweep Elections," *Radio Free Europe Research*, April 21, 1989.

[26] *Tiesa*, April 11, 1989.

Soviets in 1939 and that these would be denounced.[27] Subsequently, in the same paper, the chairman of Lithuania's Supreme Soviet indicated the possibility of a new status for Lithuania's Communist Party and hinted at "party pluralism." The chairman also said that if the Supreme Soviet in Vilnius were to reconsider the declaration of republican sovereignty that it had failed to pass on November 18, 1988, the results could be different.[28]

On May 11, all of the Baltic republics' First Secretaries participated in a Politburo meeting in Moscow. Later, Brazauskas revealed in *Tiesa* that economic self-management and the crucial events of 1939 and 1940 had been topics of discussion. Gorbachev, Brazauskas said, understood the importance of economic autonomy, and Brazauskas was certain the Politburo would act on this issue.

The day after the First Secretary had made his opinions public, Lithuania's Supreme Soviet decided to convene a session to consider amendments to a number of constitutional articles that it had avoided ratifying on November 18, 1988. Once ratified, these articles would provide the content of republican sovereignty.

On May 18, the Soviet approved all of these amendments, the chief one declaring that only laws adopted by Lithuania's Supreme Soviet, or by referendum, would be valid in Lithuania.[29] Laws or legal acts issued by the All-Union Supreme Soviet would possess validity if and when they were duly confirmed by Lithuania's body. The amended constitution also provided for Lithuanian citizenship, guaranteed all citizens rights and freedoms given in the constitution or by international laws and legal acts and stated that citizens' rights must be protected by courts. The declaration of republican sovereignty, issued separately, recalled Lithuania's independence in the 13th and 20th centuries, pointed out its illegal incorporation into the USSR as a result of the Molotov-Ribbentrop Pact and stated that the solution to Lithuania's current social and economic plight was in "regaining state sovereignty, which today is the clearly manifested goal of the Lithuanian nation and an inalienable right of nations, which can materialize only under conditions of free national self-determination."[30] The Supreme Soviet also approved a law on economic self-management, which was virtually the same as the one worked out by Sajudis representatives together with Baltic specialists in the fall of 1988. All deputies, it seems, voted for the constitutional amendments. Two voted against the declaration of republican sovereignty and three abstained.[31]

---

[27] *Ibid.*, April 21, 1989.

[28] *Ibid.*, May 3, 1989.

[29] *Ibid.*, May 19, 1989.

[30] *Ibid.*, May 24, 1989.

[31] *Ibid.*

The vote, and Sajudis's victory, was overwhelming. Thus the Supreme Soviet of Lithuania had approved amendments to the constitution urged upon it by Sajudis half a year before. It accepted economic self-management, the Baltic economic model worked out in September of 1988 and endorsed by Sajudis's congress a month later but subsequently rejected by Moscow. The declaration on sovereignty, as phrased by the Supreme Soviet in May, was just as radical as the declaration of spiritual independence made by Sajudis on February 16. In three months, from mid-February to mid-May, Lithuania's Communist Party had moved beside the flank of Sajudis.

What were the reasons for this change? Some answers come from Sajudis's leaders. Romualdas Ozolas, a leader of the popular movement, has pointed out that the authorities simply "had no other choice but to do what was needed by all."[32] In other words, the Party submitted to a very strong majority that had expressed its demands in the March elections. There were other, specific reasons. The Party in Lithuania comprehended that the popular movement that initially had formed to advance *perestroika* had changed into a force for national rebirth whose goal was sovereignty. Further, Moscow had been negative about Lithuania's moves toward economic independence, rebuffing Lithuania's government on the four separate occasions that government had approached it. "We constantly feel resistance from central management institutions," First Secretary Brazauskas said on June 24, 1989.[33] *Perestroika* was moving slowly; it was entirely possible that the old dogmatism would recapture power in Moscow and resume the old, assimilationist nationality policies. In mid-1989, the immediate circumstances were such that Moscow could be pushed—and needed to be. When Estonia had declared its republican sovereignty in November, 1988, the Politburo had threatened it with repercussions, but these had never come. Instead, the Estonian stand had given that republic respectful attention from the entire world. Lithuania's Communists had been brought to the realization that they had to demonstrate initiative, activity and support for the cause of independence. Only thus could they retain a degree of credibility.

The low repute of the Party among the Lithuanian people was public knowledge. Newspapers revealed its weak status and role. Opinion polls conducted by a group of specialists from Lithuania's Academy of Sciences showed that Sajudis received a rating of 68 points (from a possible 100) and that the Communist Party of Lithuania received only 22 points. Yet on the same scale, First Secretary Brazauskas was given 84 points, 14 more than Vytautas Landsbergis, the president of Sajudis, and 21 more than Gor-

---

[32] *Ibid.*, May 21, 1989.
[33] *Ibid.*, June 25, 1989.

bachev.[34] Brazauskas's public display of activism was obviously paying off. There now were suggestions that the Lithuanian Party detach itself from the Communist Party of the Soviet Union, which then would be reconstituted as an association of Communist parties from each of the republics, and that the Communists retreat from the position that their Party must possess the "leading role," thereby also admitting the existence of other political parties. The Academy of Sciences prepared a new draft constitution, which Sajudis reviewed, explicitly rejecting the Party's primacy in the political system.[35] The Secretary of the Kaunas Party organization wrote that a multiparty system would much better allow the expression of diverse groups' political interests. He thought that the time had come to prepare a *modus vivendi* whereby the Communists could collaborate, or coexist, with other political forces in a parliamentary setting.[36]

While the secession of the local Party from the All-Union one was still being discussed, other Lithuanian organizations actually proceeded to separate from the central ones. In June, Lithuania's Komsomol departed; henceforth it would be Lithuania's Communist Youth Association. The writers, artists and members of other creative professions whose organizations were branches of central ones separated from the Moscow-controlled bodies and set up their own, receiving legal status as independent organizations in Lithuania. Under the conditions of widening freedom, new associations and organizations emerged and multiplied in number. So did newspapers and publications. Ties with Lithuanian emigrants in the West, particularly in the US and Canada, were sought and strengthened.

The Lithuanian Communist Party was entering its time of troubles. In 1988, Gorbachev had moved the reluctant Party toward *perestroika*. In 1989, the Lithuanian Communists, buffeted by the wide and powerful currents of the popular movement, had to deal with their role in state and society and with their relationship to the Communist Party of the Soviet Union. When the Lithuanian Central Committee met in its plenum on June 24, 1989, it indicated, prudently, that the Party would remain faithful to the principles of socialism as defined by Lenin and would ask for autonomy, not independence, from the All-Union Party.[37] However, it should be recalled that although First Secretary Brazauskas had condemned demands for Party autonomy in the fall of 1988, less than a year later he had accepted the necessity for discussing this issue. Forces the Party no longer could control were propelling it toward the border of independence.

---

[34] *Komjaunimos Tiesa*, June 16, 1989.

[35] *Universitas Vilniensis* (No. 12, 1989), cited in *Gimtasis Krastas*, May 25–31, 1989, 3.

[36] *Kauno Tiesa* (No. 98, 1989), cited in *Gimtasis Krastas*, May 25–31, 1989, 3.

[37] *Tiesa*, June 28, 1989.

Moscow, of course, had been growing apprehensive about the Lithuanian Party moving beyond its control. Yet its apprehension about the Lithuanian drive toward national independence was much greater. Ideologically, the secession of Lithuania and the other two Baltic states, their flight from Marxism-Leninism, would demonstrate its utter failure. Politically, the three republics' secession would have profound consequences on foreign policy, badly damaging the image of the Soviet Union, and it would have no less profound effects on domestic policy, encouraging popular movements in other republics. Furthermore, despite all its talk about economic decentralization, Moscow does not want to hand over control of the economy to anyone else.

Gorbachev's position on the nationalities question has become rigid. On July 1, 1989, the General Secretary addressed the people of the Soviet Union on this issue, warning that conflicts among nationalities held a tremendous danger for the Soviet Union. Such conflicts, he said, would jeopardize *perestroika*; they could even cause the dissolution of the entire Soviet state. Gorbachev used the violent clashes in Caucasus and Central Asia as an example and did not specifically refer to the Baltic popular movements, but his words clearly implied his opposition to Baltic independence. To him, all regions of the Soviet Union were closely interconnected: cutting these connections meant "cutting up a living body." The needs of the Soviet empire stood above economic reform and modernization in the Baltic.[38]

There are great similarities between this first stage of events in Lithuania and the "Prague Spring" of 1968 in Czechoslovakia. Sajudis, along with the other Baltic popular movements, has placed Moscow in a difficult situation akin to the one it faced in 1968. Should it use all means at hand to compel Lithuania (and Estonia and Latvia) to remain in the Soviet Union? Or should it content itself with influence, instead of imperial control, over the Baltic states? The lines along which the issue must be resolved in Lithuania have been clearly drawn. On May 13–14, 1989, in Tallinn, Estonia, Sajudis made public commitments to independence together with the other Baltic popular movements, following its commitments with a mass drive for a petition demanding that Moscow abolish the consequences of the Molotov-Ribbentrop Pact, withdraw its "occupation forces" from the Baltic states and agree that the Baltic peoples should determine what political and social systems they are to have. The document was addressed to the Soviet Union; both Germanys, West and East; and the United Nations.

---

[38] *New York Times*, July 2, 1989; *Tiesa*, July 2, 1989. For Baltic attitudes toward CPSU views, see Dzintra Bungs, "Initial Baltic Reaction to CPSU Criticism," *Radio Free Europe Research*, September 11, 1989.

Gorbachev has also taken an unequivocal position, declaring that those who demand Lithuania's secession are people consumed by personal ambition or "simply extremists" who do not support socialism. In May, after the Baltic popular movements met in Tallinn, *Pravda* condemned their independence declaration as "a march forward into the past" and wrote of sovereignty as an "anachronism" and of confederation as an "obsolete" form of government.[39] Meanwhile, Lithuania's Communists stand between Moscow and Sajudis, their political standing and very legitimacy dependent on future developments. An offer of economic independence and, possibly, Gorbachev's willingness to define a "special" place for the Baltic republics in the Soviet Union would give the Communists some standing in Lithuania. Sajudis, however, would probably see such a "special" status as the first step toward independence, which now is its clear aim.

---

[39] *Pravda*, May 22, 1989.

3

The Sources of Latvia's
Popular Movement

Jan Arveds Trapans

The Popular Fronts of Latvia and Estonia and Sajudis of Lithuania have astonished the West and the Kremlin. On August 24, 1989, the *Financial Times* wrote that "in full view of fascinated yet agonised world opinion" these popular forces were moving toward a cataclysmic collision with Moscow. This clash could be avoided (so the London newspaper advised) if the Baltic people were disabused of all illusions about the West embarking on World War III to secure their freedom. Gorbachev, continued the *Financial Times*, should equally well understand that if he sent Soviet armor into the Baltic such a ruthless use of military force would wipe out all of his gains in the West and, possibly, Gorbachev himself. *Perestroika* would end, détente would collapse, the Cold War would return.[1] This is a dramatic view of events. Some six months earlier, however, the *Financial Times* and other Western newspapers contemplated the Baltic as an area for Gorbachev's economic experiments, wrote of the Popular Fronts as engines of *perestroika* and characterized their leaders as energetic—if sometimes unruly—innovators eyeing future reforms.

The Popular Fronts have changed. They probably have not changed as much as the Western press would have it, but changed they have, in political aims, methods and momentum. Sajudis's full name, Lietuvos Persitvarkymos Sajudis or "Lithuania's *Perestroika* Movement," adopted in 1988, no longer fits. A strong surge of radicalism is pushing all three Baltic movements forward, beyond reform and *perestroika*, into national political activism with the goal of independence. There are radicals and moderates in the Popular Front. (Conservative or reactionary organizations and individuals—there is no shortage of them in Latvia—who want to

---

[1] *Financial Times*, August 30, 1989.

retain political structures shaped by Brezhnev or revert to those of Stalin, have stayed away from the Popular Front.) A contest between the radicals and the moderates has shaped the policy of Latvia's popular movement from 1988 onward. We shall deal with the evolution of the Popular Front, referring frequently to this rivalry.

Latvia's radicals have been active since 1986, their organizations shaped by an open conflict with Soviet authorities. Working both outside the Popular Front and within it, the radicals have established various groups that, on occasion, have argued among themselves. Nevertheless, they have maintained, from the outset, a remarkable ability to continue their alliance, marching separately toward the same major goal—independence.[2]

Until mid-1989, a very simple demand distinguished what is "radical" in Latvia from what is not: the demand that Latvia again become an independent state, nothing less. The moderate movement, which emerged in the spring of 1988, desired to exploit *perestroika* and *glasnost* to gain broad autonomy for Latvia, and asked for "republican sovereignty." In all Baltic publications, demands have been made for "economic independence," for "republican sovereignty" and for plain "independence." These terms sound quite synonymous in English, but they are not. They designate distinct political stands taken by various groups within the Popular Fronts. Only "independence," *neatkariba* in Latvian, means leaving the Soviet Union decisively and permanently. A measure of radical power within the Popular Front can be seen in how fast and how far it has been able to move this organization from concerns with *perestroika* or "republican sovereignty" toward the demand for independence.

Latvian radicals first came to the astonished attention of the West with three mass demonstrations in 1987—the first not only in the Baltic but in the entire Soviet Union. They inspired later demonstrations in Estonia and Lithuania.[3] The Popular Fronts now use the mass demonstration, carefully timed and controlled, as a strong but peaceful means of asserting their power. The mass "human chain across the Baltic" of August 23, 1989, elicited the aforementioned agonized reassessment from the *Financial Times* as to where the Baltic movements could be heading.

---

[2] For a summary of how the various popular movements emerged, see Juris Dreifelds, "Latvian National Rebirth," *Problems of Communism*, XXXVIII (July–August, 1989), 77–79; V. Stanley Vardys, "Lithuanian National Politics," *ibid.*, 53–76; and Rein Taagepera, "Estonia in September 1988: Stalinists, Centrists and Restorationists," *Journal of Baltic Studies*, XX (Summer, 1989), 175–190.

[3] See Radio Free Europe Latvian Language Service, Record of Interview (June 15, 1987); Dzintra Bungs, "The Latvian Demonstration of 23 August 1987," *Radio Free Europe Research*, October 28, 1987; and Dzintra Bungs, "A Survey of Demonstrations on November 18," *ibid.*, December 18, 1987.

The first Latvian radical organization to gain recognition in the West was Helsinki-86 (or the Organization for the Defense of Human Rights Helsinki-86) founded by a group of workers in the city of Liepaja in 1986 to secure rights proclaimed in the Helsinki Accords. The founders sent carefully composed and painstakingly handwritten documents to major Western statesmen and organizations. When read in retrospect, we find in them the genesis of current radical positions: political and economic autonomy, a respect for human rights, the end of russification and the recognition of Latvian as the official, or state, language. Later such demands would be carefully studied in the West; in 1986 no one took notice.[4] The KGB, however, did. Helsinki-86 members were harassed and arrested. They decided to make a bold move and called for a demonstration at Riga's Monument of Liberty on June 14, 1987, to commemorate the Soviet mass deportations of 1941.[5] Contrary to expectations, the demonstration succeeded.

Many descriptions of this event have found their way to the West. An image drawn by one of those who stood at the base of the monument—although no doubt, oversimplified—provides the essentials of what happened and foretells the future. Demonstrators, the curious and a scattering of hostile officials stood in concentric rings around the monument. Helsinki-86 leaders knelt silently and placed flowers beneath the inscription "For Fatherland and Freedom," then gave short speeches. Among the outer rings of spectators were scattered most of Riga's intellectual elite: writers, artists, professionals, poets—excited, curious, embarrassed not to be at the heart of the demonstration. Much could be told (so claims the observer) by how far someone stood from the monument and when and if he broke loose from his spot to move toward it. Some did; many more hesitated. The demonstrators did not disperse until late in the night and came back the next day and for days afterwards. Photographs show that the

---

[4] The Latvian Human Rights Organization Helsinki-86 was founded with the intention of submitting documents to a joint Soviet-American Chautauque conference, held in the city of Jurmala, Latvia, in July, 1986. The organizers failed to reach the conference but their documents found their way to the West. The following declarations, written in July (and translated and disseminated by the American Latvian Association, Washington, D.C.), are of importance: "To the US Delegation at Jurmala Conference," "Charter Document of Helsinki-86," "To the United Nations" and "To the Central Committee of the Communist Party of the USSR and the Latvian SSR." A review of the conference is given in Dzintra Bungs, "Imperfect Glasnost," *Radio Free Europe Research*, December 9, 1987.

[5] Helsinki-86 distributed leaflets announcing the proposed demonstration: see "Statement on Commemorating June 14" (June 9, 1987) and "Demonstration in Latvia Commemorating Mass Deportations" (June 13, 1987).

base of the monument was covered with mounds of flowers, deep as snowdrifts. Militia would sweep these away surreptitiously, under the cover of darkness.[6]

On June 14, a crack had opened in the façade of Soviet control over the Baltic. The rest of the year was punctuated by successive demonstrations, deepening the fissure. On August 23, a demonstration marking the Molotov-Ribbentrop Pact of 1939 pointed out that the Baltic states had become part of the Soviet Union by secrecy, force and against their will; on November 18, Latvia's declaration of independence was commemorated—a public defiance of Soviet rule that even in 1987 was close to treason. The KGB fought against the demonstrations with harassment and arrest, and by expelling Helsinki-86 leaders to the West. November 18 saw a bloody clash at the Monument of Liberty in Riga and in other cities, causing a group of US senators to warn Gorbachev that his tolerance for peaceful demonstrations would be considered the test of his sincerity in *glasnost*. Demonstrations also broke out in Estonia and Lithuania.[7]

The 1987 demonstrations in which the Latvian radicals had fought off the Party were subsequently called the "calendar riots." The reference is historical: during the Reformation in Riga, there had been "calendar riots" during which artisans and journeymen had sacked churches, chased bishops and assaulted the "well-fed and sleek" clergy for, they said, parading idolatry and celebrating false saint's days in the calendar; they would celebrate the true ones.

Although Helsinki-86 was the first radical organization to gain attention in the West, the Latvian Greens, or, properly, the Club for the Defense of the Environment (Vides Aizsardzibas Klubs, or VAK), were the first among the informal groups from which radicals would emerge.[8] Perceptible as a

---

[6] On the June 14 demonstration, see Radio Free Europe Latvian Language Service, Report of a Participant (June 16, 1987).

[7] Soviet official response to the June 14 demonstrations was uncertain, attempting to criticize and minimize the event at the same time. Five days after the demonstration, Mavriks Vulfsons, a senior political commentator, presented the interpretation that Helsinki-86 was a misguided group incited by Western broadcasts; nonetheless, demonstrations *per se* were not to be condemned: *Rigas Balss*, June 19, 1987. Vulfsons would change his stance and emerge as a major leader of the popular movements in 1988. On the subsequent demonstrations of August 23, see *Cina*, August 25, 1987, and *Padomju Jaunatne*, August 26, 1987. However, much the best evidence on these events will be found in video recordings, made surreptitiously and brought to the West. See also Dzintra Bungs, "One-and-a-Half Years of Helsinki-86," *Radio Free Europe Research*, February 16, 1988.

[8] Nils Muiznieks, "The Daugavpils Hydro Station and 'Glasnost' in Latvia," *Journal of Baltic Studies*, XVIII (Spring, 1987), 63.

strong movement in 1986, VAK was officially consolidated as an organization in 1987. Dainis Ivans, president of Latvia's Popular Front, has said: "In Latvia everything began with the movement to save the environment. The Club . . . was founded. Individual fighters arose, prophets. The great awakening had begun."[9] The incipient Green movement won its first battle by stopping a huge hydroelectric dam project in 1986. A small Latvian David had demolished Moscow's centralized-planning Goliath and thus gained immediate prestige. In the summer of 1988, the Greens continued demonstrating for the environment, but the brunt of their efforts was distinctly political. All major political meetings of 1988 had the Greens at the center as organizers and leaders.[10]

Today the largest and most powerful radical movement—with more than 10,000 dues-paying members in the fall of 1989—is the Latvian National Independence Movement (Latvijas Nacionala Neatkaribas Kustiba, or LNNK), founded on June 18, 1988.[11] The Movement is led by a collective council of 15 members and has no single executive officer, although its most distinguished leader is Eduards Berklavs. A former Party member, Berklavs was dismissed as Latvia's Deputy Prime Minister and Party Secretary in 1959 by Nikita Khrushchev. Charged with "bourgeois nationalism," he was exiled from Latvia and subsequently expelled from the Party. In 1959, Berklavs had attempted to implement an economic and political policy that, in its basic outlines, resembled "economic sovereignty" demands under *perestroika*. With Berklavs's fall, centralization, russification and retrograde Stalinism dominated Latvia, and the year 1959 is considered a tragic turning point in Latvia's post-war history.[12] Berklavs's repute and political sagacity, a young and energetic membership and the word "independence" in the official name of the organization quickly advanced the Movement as the leading force in radical politics by the end of 1988.

---

[9] Dreifelds, "Latvian National Rebirth," 81n.

[10] The Green movement is described in Vita Terauda, *The Rise of Grass Roots Environmental Groups under Gorbachev: A Case Study of Latvia* (Washington, D.C.: Johns Hopkins University SAIS, 1988).

[11] Dzintra Bungs, "New Group for Latvian Independence Formed," *Radio Free Europe Research*, July 13, 1988, and *Neatkariba* (September, 1988), 2–3.

[12] Eduards Berklavs (b. 1917), a Party member from 1939 to 1973, attempted to reassert Latvian control over the republic while deputy chairman of the Council of Ministers from 1954 to 1956 and from 1958 to 1959. His successor in determining the Party's policy in Latvia was Arvids Pelse, a rigid Stalinist who introduced russification and centralization. Berklavs's biography was reviewed in the prestigious weekly *Literatura un maksla* on July 15, 1988. The entire record of the crucial events of 1959 was published in 1989 by the Party monthly: *Padomju Latvijas Komunists* (February), 78–94; (March), 80–95; (April), 79–95; (May), 79–95; and (June), 63–95.

The fourth important radical organization in Latvia is Renaissance and Renewal (Atdzimsana un atjaunosanas). This is a religious movement with an immediate concern for reviving the Lutheran church, which, in the eyes of some clergymen, served the state with great diligence but served God very little.[13] Led by two outstanding personalities, Modris Plate and Juris Rubenis, Renewal has fought a series of determined encounters with Communist officials and elderly and complaisant clergy. The organization won a culminating battle when the clerical radicals ousted the incumbent archbishop. A new synod was elected along with a new archbishop, Karlis Gailitis, who, in his first speech, emphasized that he was a member of the Latvian National Independence Movement. Both Plate and Rubenis, particularly the latter, were central figures and speakers in the major radical demonstrations of 1988.[14]

These four radical organizations and other, smaller, ones that have not been described all sprang to life between 1986 and early 1988. Members and, particularly, leaders of these organizations then risked, at best, arrest and beating or, at worst, prison and forced-labor camp. Helsinki-86's two key activists first met in a shared KGB prison cell early in 1987. In the early stages of the radical movements, former political prisoners joined up. Some of the first young recruits dropped everyday employment to live for their cause. Such militants are easily recognizable figures in political history: they are brave and intransigent, dedicated and intolerant; to them compromise is akin to treason. These radical traits have diminished as various organizations have gathered new members by the thousands, but they continue to exist. The radical movements still bear some traces of their underground origins, of persecution and prison.

The radical actions of 1987 were the first sources from which Latvia's popular movement would flow. The second were the activities of the "creative intelligentsia," who would come to lead the moderate wing of the movement. The intellectuals already belonged to organizations—the "creative unions," which had been established by the Party to corral and control creative minds. Under the conditions of expanding *perestroika*, the unions could be used for different purposes—even to criticize the Party. The creative unions had their own publications. They also had counterparts in

---

[13] Documents and descriptions of how Atdzimsana un atjaunosanas was formed are found in the Helsinki-86 publication *Auseklis* (October–November, 1987): Garidznieku grupa Atdzimsana un atjaunosanas, "Dokuments Nr. 1, Informacija par grupas dibinasanu un merkiem," 85–86; "Dokuments Nr. 3, Kristigas kustibas Atdzimsana un atjaunosanas pamatprincipi," 88–89; and "Latviesu luterani krustcelos," 91–95.

[14] Radio Free Europe Latvian Language Service, Interview (April 12, 1989); and *Atmoda*, April 30, 1989.

Estonia and Lithuania about which they had much personal knowledge. In addition, they could draw on a tradition of intellectual dissent in the Baltic, regularly expressed in literature and art and just as regularly suppressed by the Party. The intellectuals did more than just express curiosity about the radical demonstrations. On March 3, 1988, the creative unions' executive boards called for a discussion of the "tragic consequences" of Stalinism and how intellectuals could deal with them.[15] The moving force on this occasion, as on subsequent ones, was Janis Peters, chairman of the Writers' Union.

As the intellectuals deliberated, Helsinki-86 worked toward one more demonstration, set for March 25, 1988, to mark the second Soviet mass deportation in 1949.[16] This time the creative unions announced that they themselves would organize the memorial occasion, not at Riga's Monument of Liberty but at Latvia's national cemetery, the Cemetery of the Brethren, a place almost as symbolic as the monument but located, conveniently, on the outskirts of the city. Helsinki-86 charged that the intellectuals had been prodded by the Party to upstage them; the creative unions spoke of their desire to honor victims of Stalinism. It is possible that both claims were true. The ceremony at the cemetery was widely promoted and drew tens of thousands of participants. The memorial organized by Helsinki-86 attracted thousands.

March 25 marked the end of repressions. Henceforth demonstrations would be legal. The KGB would no longer attempt to destroy radical organizations by expelling their leaders abroad; there would be no more beatings, arrests or imprisonments for political activities. March 25 also marked the arrival of the intellectuals and the moderates, the second source from which a current would flow toward the Popular Front. The intellectuals had organized a large and peaceful demonstration against Stalinism. The Party would accept them as organizers of a large and peaceful movement for *perestroika*.

The impulse for a Popular Front came from Estonia.[17] Its genesis, perhaps, can be seen in the meeting of Estonia's creative unions on April 1 and 2, 1988; some three weeks later Edgar Savisaar, an economist who soon emerged as a leader of the popular movement, promoted the idea for a Popular Front in a Tallinn television broadcast. The notion of a Popular

---

[15] *Literatura un maksla*, March 18, 1988.

[16] *Ibid.*, March 31, 1988. The most telling evidence of the event is a video recording made by members of Helsinki-86. Some three hours long, it contains many interviews recorded during the ceremony and excellently conveys the feelings of that day.

[17] Toomas Ilves, "Cultural Unions Adopt Resolution on Nationality Reforms," *Radio Free Europe Research*, June 3, 1988.

Front that would link the broad opportunity of *perestroika* with the need to solve local concerns was picked up first by the Lithuanians and later, somewhat more hesitantly, by the Latvians.[18]

Latvia's creative intelligentsia met on June 1 and 2, 1988, in an "extended plenum" of the Writers' Union, a signal event in the formation of the republic's Popular Front.[19] Speeches given at the plenum contained broad indictments of economic and social ills and proposed recognition of Latvia as a distinct entity within a Soviet federation with sovereign rights over republican affairs, a law of republican citizenship and recognition of Latvian as the state language. The speeches were published after the plenum.[20] They contained the moderates' political program; concentrated and summarized they would be presented at the founding congress of the Front. Some demands were similar to the ones radicals had already voiced but more modest in intent. To the intellectuals, "republican sovereignty" meant local autonomy, achieved primarily by economic measures and within an overall context of *perestroika*. To the radicals, "sovereignty" meant one step short of independence, a step that was to be taken not through economic maneuvering but by political action.

At the June plenum, the creative intelligentsia also asked that the record be set straight on the events of August, 1939, and June, 1940, that destroyed Latvia as a state and on the mass deportations of June, 1941, and March, 1949, which severely damaged the Latvian nation.[21] Mavriks Vulfsons, an old party member recognized as one of the most experienced and circumspect of Soviet journalists, spoke on 1940. No "socialist revolution" had taken place in Latvia, Vulfsons said. He had been a Party activist then; he knew. Vulfsons's statement shocked the Party more than any other issued at the congress: it challenged the Party's claim to rule legitimately.

On June 14, 1988, the environmental movement, assisted by Helsinki-86, organized a mass rally to commemorate, again, the deportations of June 14, 1941. The authorities gave official sanction for the meeting, evidently assuming that the thrust of protest would be directed toward the past and Stalinist crimes, as on March 25. But the Party had miscalculated badly. At the meeting, which was followed by a march to the Monument of Liberty, speakers made political demands directed toward the future and marchers

---

[18] Vardys, "Lithuanian National Politics," 56–57.

[19] For an outline of the issues presented at the plenum, see *Literatura un maksla*, June 10, 1988.

[20] The speeches given at the plenum were subsequently printed in *Literatura un maksla* in the June 10 and 17, July 1 and 8 issues.

[21] *Ibid.*

carried the still-forbidden red-white-red flag of independent Latvia.[22] Four days later, a plenum of the Latvian Communist Party Central Committee took place. The record of the discussion (never published in Latvia, but available in the West) is a register of confusion, rage and recriminations.[23] There were calls that Ideological Secretary Anatolijs Gorbunovs resign (he had, unhappily, been present at the mass gathering on June 14) along with vituperation against old Party member Vulfsons (a "political prostitute"). First Secretary Boris Pugo found comfort in the presence of Soviet tanks. Bewildered, the Party sought to comprehend what forces were breaking loose in Latvia. Throughout the plenum, the question on all minds was: "What next?"

Even as the Central Committee members were assembling for their plenum, the Latvian National Independence Movement was being founded, on June 17.[24] Reflecting upon the developments in the summer and fall of 1988 in his own country, an Estonian would later write: "At first nobody wanted to say the word 'independence' for fear of Moscow's reaction. But then somebody said 'I' and nothing happened. Eventually someone blurted out the entire word."[25] Though the "entire word" was written in the Latvian National Independence Movement's name, its program was more prudent, demanding immediate sovereign powers over all affairs of the republic but indicating that actual independence was a matter for the future. Present at the Movement's founding were the most prominent radicals—members of Helsinki-86, the Greens and other groups. They wanted to have an organization that was national and democratic in nature and had a clear political aim. The core of the Movement's initial program had already been stated by Eduards Berklavs, in his speech on June 14, to tens of thousands of listeners.

---

[22] Radio Free Europe Latvian Language Service, Interview with a Participant (June 21, 1988). As in the case of other major events, the best evidence available comes from a video recording, made by a Helsinki-86 member.

[23] The transcript, "Plenum of the Central Committee of the Latvian Communist Party, June 17, 1988," was made by a participant and disseminated in Riga. Its authenticity has not been questioned by Western scholars. The Party did not publish its own transcript, although demands to do so repeatedly appeared in Latvia's press. A summary of the transcript was published in *Baltic Forum* VI (Fall, 1988). Interesting evidence of the indignant response to the plenum in a public meeting (the plenum's content having become generally known in Riga) is "Protesta mitins Preses nama," *Auseklis* (1988: IV), 28–32.

[24] *Neatkariba* (1988: I), 2–3, published a revealing summary of the debates of the founders of the Movement about the aims of the organization. See also Dzintra Bungs, "New Group for Latvian Independence Formed," *Radio Free Europe Research*, July 13, 1988.

[25] *International Herald Tribune*, August 28, 1989.

Our first duty [Berklavs had said] is to declare outright that the mass deportations . . . were a planned crime, directed deliberately toward the destruction of Latvia as a nation. . . . Stalin and all of his successors up to Mikhail Gorbachev have intended to destroy the Latvian nation.[26]

Further, he had demanded:

We must make certain that the Latvians regain their national sovereignty, that the Latvian language is the official state language, and that there is a law of citizenship. There must be an end to a worthless, ecologically damaging expansion of industry that has murdered Latvia's nature, befouled our streams, lakes and the very sea itself. The government does not like that we talk of this but we must—there is no indication that the government has decided to act.[27]

Finally—to loud ovations—Berklavs had stated that if the government was "unwilling or unable to fulfill its functions," it must surrender its right to govern.[28]

From June to September, radicals and moderates wrestled and pushed each other toward organizing the Popular Front—radicals now guided by Berklavs and speaking the language of politics and moderates guided by Janis Peters, who still wrote of the importance of *perestroika* and carefully outlined an economic road toward the political goal of republican sovereignty. There were huge meetings and rallies—now held with a relative impunity from authorities—demanding the legalization of independent Latvia's flag, the revelation and punishment of Stalinist crimes and the closing down of huge plants governed from Moscow that were destroying Latvia's nature. These demonstrations were largely but no longer entirely dominated by the radicals, while a series of long, programmatic articles in Latvian newspapers were usually, but not exclusively, signed by the moderates.

On June 21, an Organizing Committee for a Popular Front issued a proclamation signed by a number of prominent radicals. A few days later, another proclamation was issued with virtually the same text but with different signatures—those of prominent moderates.[29] Dainis Ivans, later the president of the Front, whose name appeared on both documents, explained somewhat lamely that "evidently someone did not like the names

---

[26] Video recording of June 14 meeting.

[27] *Ibid.*

[28] *Ibid.*

[29] Dreifelds, "Latvian National Rebirth," 84; and "Sabiedrisko grupu parstavji aicina," *Auseklis* (1989: IV).

and the organizations" on the first document.[30] The evident "someone" was clearly Janis Peters, the moderate leader who used the resources of the creative unions for the formation of the Front. Matters were spurred forward in June but then lagged; in September there appeared an "Informal Popular Front," another radical organization (later it would be reconstituted as the "Radical Alliance" within the Front).[31] In their push to organize a Front, both groups attempted to outflank each other, but the moderates, although moving more slowly, had the advantage of their large, existing organizations, access to newspapers and, finally, when matters moved far enough, permission from the Party to organize a congress on October 8 and 9.

The Party's decision had been made earlier, by Moscow. In August, Aleksandr Yakovlev, Gorbachev's adviser and expert on the Baltic, traveled to Riga and from there to Vilnius. Yakovlev talked to the leading minds of the creative unions and the moderate leaders. The content of these meetings was widely reported in the press. Yakovlev also talked to local Party leaders, but these conversations were reported on sparsely.[32] What conclusions he drew he took back to Gorbachev; of these we know nothing. But subsequent events indicate what they might have been. Before the Popular Front congresses took place, the First Secretaries of the Latvian and Lithuanian parties were dismissed and replaced by younger men, supporters of *perestroika*. (Estonia's First Secretary had been dismissed earlier.) Probably, Gorbachev chose the popular movements over the local parties as forces that would build *perestroika*. Publicly, he would give the Popular Fronts such praise. If indeed Gorbachev made a decision for the Fronts, as seems likely, this was both a turning point for the Baltic and a mistake by Moscow. Within a few months, all three Baltic Popular Fronts had gone far beyond the modest confines of *glasnost* and *perestroika*.

From June to October, 1988, Latvia's political stage was one in which the two figures of radicalism and moderation advanced toward the center against a background of increasingly larger and more resonant demonstrations. The third figure, standing closer to the wings, was the Communist Party. Much distraught by unexpected events, as the record of its Central Committee plenum shows, it had not recovered its bearings. In an article published later in the Party's theoretical monthly *Padomju Latvijas Komunists*

---

[30] Dreifelds, "Latvian National Rebirth," 84.

[31] The origins of the Front are described in Dzintra Bungs, "Popular Front Planned," *Radio Free Europe Research*, July 13, 1988.

[32] Concerning the moderate and radical responses to Moscow and the Popular Front, see "Aleksandrs Nikolajevics Riga," *Auseklis* (1988: VII), 19–21; and Dzintra Bungs, "Yakovlev in Latvia: An Exercise in 'Socialist Pluralism,'" *Radio Free Europe Research*, August 26, 1988.

(*Soviet Latvian Communist*), its author wrote of "the hot summer of 1988" in which "events to a certain extent resembled the maturing of a revolutionary situation" (here the author referred to Lenin's definition of what revolutions are about) that mounted in intensity until "the political activity of the workers—the third revolutionary requirement—received its most vivid confirmation on October 7, the immense meeting in favor of democratization."[33] On that day, the radicals mounted their greatest demonstration of 1988 to inaugurate the congress of the Popular Front, which began the following day.

The congress took place in Riga, where some thousand delegates, elected or selected from various organizations (including all the radical ones), deliberated on the meaning, structure and program of the new organization. The proceedings were broadcast on Latvian television and radio and thoroughly covered by the Western press. There was much emotion and much confusion. All speakers who were bold and fervent were tumultuously applauded, even when they contradicted each other. The congress reiterated many of the points made in the plenum of the creative unions of June 1 and 2, which now were recast as resolutions. It asked that privileges of Party members be abolished; there was also much talk about *perestroika* and a demand for Latvian "economic sovereignty." The overall program of the Front was shaped by the moderates.[34]

There was some disappointment among the radicals after the congress. They had held their own debate on the floor, but the agenda of the congress, its conduct and, finally, its outcome had been largely in moderate hands. In June, when the young Latvian National Independence Movement had first considered the political significance of a Popular Front, the Movement's leadership had been concerned about the possibility that the Front could be controlled by "the bureaucratic forces," that much of its drive first could be directed into the existing structures of the creative unions and, once tamed, shifted toward reformist channels. And indeed, though a considerable number of radicals had been elected to the governing bodies of the new Popular Front, they had not scored a victory.[35]

In a thoughtful article on the internal composition and dynamics of the Front published in one of the earlier issues of *Atmoda* (*Awakening*), its official weekly, Janis Freimanis (a professor, a moderate and subsequently the chairman of the executive board) charted the structure of the Front in

---

[33] V. Bluzma, "'Neformali': kas tie ir?" *Padomju Latvijas Komunists* (June, 1988), 54–57.

[34] The founding congress was recorded by Latvian television Ñagain, the best evidence available.

[35] Radio Free Europe Latvian Language Service, Record of Interviews (October 10 and 12, 1988), and Transcript, Press Conference, October 10, 1988.

terms of political blocs. The article assumed that Party members had
entered one wing of the Front and the radicals the other in order to establish
their camps: the center was taken by moderates—professionals and intellectuals. The article implied that the Party would form a consolidated bloc,
a pressure group, while the radicals would act as discrete, free-floating
individuals. The author assumed that radical organizations within the
Front would dissolve and turn to their proper concerns outside it: the
Greens to nature, Renaissance and Reformation to God. Helsinki-86 could
wither away. The Party, of course, would not wither.[36]

The Party breathed more easily after the congress, believing that everything, after all, could be contained. Gorbachev had said that the Baltic
organizations were a positive force in the restructuring movement, and
Baltic Party dignitaries noted that their single-party system could accommodate the new independent associations. The Communists, led by First
Secretary Janis Vagris, hoped that the dangerous forces let loose by the hot
summer of 1988 had been spent, and that the Party and the popular
movement could coexist under a flag of truce.[37]

The truce did not last long. Within a few weeks, there was animosity
between the Baltic Communist parties and Fronts. The first blow was
delivered against economic separatism. Late in September, moderate economic experts had met in Riga to plan Baltic economic autonomy. Moscow
found such plans deplorable; when, in November, Gorbachev suggested
amendments to the Soviet Constitution and outlined provisions for the
new Congress of People's Deputies and the new Supreme Soviet, he
proposed that the sovereign rights the republics possessed be reduced and
their representation in the new central bodies diminished.

Representatives of all three Baltic movements met in Riga on November 8. They made a joint statement opposing the proposed constitutional
amendments, outlining legal guarantees for economic autonomy and
appealing to the Baltic populations to sign a mass petition supporting their
stand. In response, Moscow sent three Politburo members to the Baltic:
Chebrikov, Slyunkov and Medvedev. In Estonia, Chebrikov put the case
bluntly: *perestroika* had been introduced to strengthen the unity of the state.
Latvia's radicals jeered that Moscow had sent "new Zhdanovs, Vyshinskis
and Dekanozovs" to the Baltic (naming Stalin's special emissaries of 1940).[38]

A second political clash followed. On November 17, Estonia's Supreme
Soviet amended the republic's constitution so that laws passed in Moscow

[36] Janis Freimanis, *Atmoda*, January 23, 1989. Freimanis further expounded his
views in articles published by *Atmoda* on March 27 and April 28.

[37] Press Conference, October 10, 1988.

[38] Radio Free Europe Latvian Language Service, Record of Interview (November 12, 1988).

became valid only after Estonia's Soviet approved them. This decision was heatedly opposed by Gorbachev. On November 18, Lithuania's Supreme Soviet was to follow the Estonian lead but balked. Latvia's Supreme Soviet ducked away completely from the decision, and the Popular Front failed to press it strongly.[39] In this event, as in others, the Front's moderates pleaded special circumstances: there were many more Russians in Latvia and in its Party. Their point was not unjustified, but it came back as a mocking echo from the radicals: after all, they said, our Front is neither Estonian nor Lithuanian; we must plead special circumstances.

The events of November provided another turning point. After the congress, moderates had spoken with much faith in *perestroika* and Gorbachev. Their disappointment was keen. Distrust toward Moscow, never far beneath the surface among the Baltic nations, was abruptly awakened. To many, the General Secretary now reappeared as a familiar figure: a Party leader who wanted to reform the empire only to strengthen it, a man with no interest in or understanding of the Baltic. Moscow's moves had done permanent damage to the moderates' notion that the Popular Fronts could reconcile their own aims and demands for broad autonomy with Gorbachev's purposes. Perceptibly, the word *"perestroika"* began to disappear from many Latvian publications.

In the winter and spring, criticism directed toward the moderates grew. On March 26, 1989, elections to the Congress of People's Deputies took place in the Baltic. In Lithuania, Sajudis scored a stunning victory. Latvia's Popular Front also did extremely well, but since there had been no explicit contests between "the Front and the Party" as in Lithuania, it was not as clear or sharp-edged a triumph. One contest in Latvia, however, captured the imagination of the country—and the world's press. Juris Dobelis, the candidate of the Latvian National Independence Movement, almost unseated First Secretary Janis Vagris. The radicals were elated. The lesson was clear: challenge and confrontation were the right roads to take. Both the moderates and the radicals could take justified satisfaction in the showing they had made in the elections. But the political appetite of the latter became keener.

The radicals' argument against the moderates is directed, they say, against their uncertain political stance and suspect social origins. Politically, the moderates ask for "economic independence" and "republican sovereignty." But even a maximum autonomy within Soviet borders would leave the Latvians within the decaying Soviet structure, where Moscow would always rule and reform controlled by Baltic movements never would be possible. The radicals are leery of the social and professional

---

[39] On the conflict, see Vardys, "Lithuanian National Politics," 45–46, and Dreifelds, "Latvian National Rebirth," 86–87.

origins of the moderates because many come from the *priviligentsia*. This intellectual and professional elite lived well enough before *perestroika* and, though it may desire a complete overhaul of the Soviet structure, doesn't want its removal because it would then lose its privileges. Thus the moderates, say the radicals, even while hoping to thwart many of the Party's political designs and despite their apparent, intermittent conflict with it, share with the Party a hidden nexus of linked interests.

The radicals' argument against the Party is directed against what they described as its dismal past and deceitful present. Communists are held responsible for all the evils that have befallen Latvia as a state and the Latvians as a nation. Beginning with the atrocities of Stalinism—executions and mass deportations; continuing with the destruction of Latvian society, countryside and traditional agrarian life through forced collectivization and russification; and ending with the Brezhnevite policy of deliberately inserting huge, inefficient industrial plants in Latvia that have brought in more Russians and left behind incredible pollution and ravaged nature: there is not, say the radicals, a single moment in Latvia's history after June, 1940, to which one could point and say, "There the Party did good!" The Communists had destroyed or befouled everything in Latvian life. Their *perestroika* was a fraud—a last-ditch effort to salvage socialism in which Latvians, Estonians and Lithuanians were being used as caulking for the seams of a decrepit boat that was inexorably sinking. To remain in the USSR, the radicals argue, was suicidal. The Latvian nation could save itself only by leaping from the boat, across the Soviet border, into freedom.

The central argument proposed by the radicals to support their demand for independence is grounded in the events of 1939 and 1940. The Baltic states, they say, lost their independence when two criminal powers signed a secret deal in 1939, the Molotov-Ribbentrop Pact. In 1940, the Soviet Union invaded the three Baltic countries and, after illegally convoking puppet assemblies, incorporated all three. There was no "socialist revolution" in the Baltic in 1940, as Moscow still continues to claim. The decisions of 1940 are null and void (as the secret protocols of 1939, from the viewpoint of international law, have been null and void from the outset). The successors of the illegal "People's Diets" of 1940, the Supreme Soviets of today, are also null and void. Today, the radicals conclude, the Baltic states are under military occupation. This, of course, is a complicated chain of reasoning, but experts on international law would agree that the radicals have a substantial case.

In the summer of 1989, the contention that Latvia was under Soviet occupation became a heated political issue. Western newspapers wrote of a commission set up in Moscow to investigate the Molotov-Ribbentrop Pact. In the Baltic states, popular television shows flaunted copies of the secret protocols with Molotov's and Ribbentrop's signatures. As the commission of experts in Moscow procrastinated, Baltic newspapers wrote of the duplicity of Soviet behavior in 1939 and in 1989. The Soviet Union had stolen the Baltic states when the two bloodiest criminals in human history made a secret and filthy deal: Moscow had to admit it, own up to the consequences, confess that its power was illegitimate.

All this was history-as-politics with a vengeance and grist for the radical mill. Public-opinion polls published in 1989 showed that all of the Baltic radical organizations had high popularity ratings, possibly not as high as the Popular Fronts' but much higher than the Communist parties'. In Latvia, radical arguments and radical control over the Popular Front increased. This was shown in May when the three Baltic Fronts met in Tallinn, Estonia. Their joint assembly adopted extremely important decisions. It indicated that the Baltic states could be independent in a neutral, demilitarized "Baltic-Scandinavia." The assembly denounced and declared null and void the Molotov-Ribbentrop Pact and appealed to foreign heads of state and international organizations to observe the aspirations of the Baltic nations for self-determination and independence. The leaders of the three Baltic movements had declared in principle for independence.[40] (There were, however, opposition to the Tallinn decision within the central bodies of Latvia's Popular Front and claims that it had been made hastily without adequate consideration.[41])

There have been other forces at work, of course, moving the leadership of the Front away from its moderate and reformist stance of October, 1988. There has been a growing distrust toward Moscow. There has been the example of the Estonian and Lithuanian movements, which have been bolder than the Latvian one. And, underneath it all, the Popular Fronts have tasted and liked power. In 1988, still organizing their movement, they had spoken and moved prudently, always glancing back at the Party. By 1989, they had won elections, they had read opinion polls indicating how popular they were and they had been interviewed by Western correspondents who found local Party functionaries dull and politically uninteresting. All this could not but give the leaders of Latvia's Front more purpose and self-confidence. The Popular Front is a grass-roots movement, with numerous and active local chapters in the countryside that are often influenced, or controlled, by the radicals; indeed the radicals have made a deliberate effort to capture them. Radical proposals have seeped upwards from their rural roots to the intellectual leaves, feeding the moderate leadership with vigorous and determined sap.

---

[40] *Padomju Jaunatne*, May 16, 1989. Full details of the Baltic proposals are given in *Padomju Jaunatne*, May 25, 1989. See also Dzintra Bungs, "Latvia in May 1989: Thinking of Independence," *Radio Free Europe Research*, July 7, 1989.

[41] Dreifelds, "Latvian National Rebirth," 88.

If the radicals and the moderates were the main actors in Latvian politics, the stage for their actions had been set, to a great extent, by Gorbachev himself—much to his own disadvantage. With *glasnost* and *perestroika*, Gorbachev inadvertently encouraged strong forces in the Baltic that turned against Moscow. *Glasnost* was supposed to mean more candor about public life and mistakes of the past; in the Baltic, it came to mean withering criticism of everything the Communist Party and the Soviet Union had done since 1940. *Perestroika* meant reforming the economy; if it is still mentioned in the Baltic, it is, at the most, viewed as a brief and transitory stage on the road to independence. Democratization, for Gorbachev, meant more power for himself and the Soviet government, so that the sluggish and reactionary Party body could be pushed aside; in the Baltic, democratization means elections won and Supreme Soviets transmuted into parliamentary platforms from which demands for independence can be made.

What future for Baltic radicalism? The future of the radicals may lie in an organization the Estonians and Latvians have been building up since February, 1989: the Citizens' Committees. The Committees were initiated in Estonia by the leading radical organizations, and the Latvian radicals followed their example. The Committees register all those who were citizens in June, 1940, and their descendants. Those registered elect delegates to a congress that will decide "the fate of the republic." The powers of the congress are based upon the argument that only the citizens of the former, independent, legal republic (and their offspring) have *de jure* rights. Those who have entered the Baltic states as officials of the "occupying power" do not. The power of the movement is based upon the fact that Latvians and Estonians are registering by the hundreds of thousands. The claim made is that they will possess legitimate, parliamentary powers as successors to the parliaments of the independent states.

In *The Anatomy of Revolution,* Crane Brinton wrote: "When another and conflicting set of institutions provides another and conflicting set of decisions, you have dual sovereignty."[42] It may be argued that the Popular Front has become an institution issuing a conflicting set of decisions against those of the old, established rule of the Party; it could be said that the radical Citizens' Committees loom in the future as an emerging institution that will challenge the old regime. In any event, the contest between the radicals and the moderates has shaped the policy and the structure of the Popular Front: the result has undermined the Communist Party and Moscow's control over Latvia.

---

[42] Crane Brinton, *The Anatomy of Revolution,* revised and expanded edition (New York: Vintage Books, 1965), 133.

4

The Popular Movements
and the Soviet Union: Discussion

The conference was fortunate indeed in having representatives from three Popular Fronts present: Marju Lauristin from Estonia's Popular Front; Eduards Berklavs, who was in the leadership of both the Latvian Popular Front and Latvia's National Independence Movement; and Yurii Badzo of Rukh, Ukraine's Popular Front, which, at the very time of the conference, had gathered in its own founding congress. The Popular Front representatives were asked first to review the immediate situation in their respective republics, then to assess the temperature and political direction of the different movements and finally to consider how Moscow would react to future moves. Throughout the year there had been convulsions in Moscow about nationalism imperiling the future of the Soviet Union.

Mr. Berklavs's point of departure was a recent statement by the Central Committee. In August, 1989, the Central Committee, fearing Baltic separatism, had threatened the three movements with "the most grievous consequences." For all that, independence had become the primary aim of the Baltic popular movements. This shift from the limited goal of republican sovereignty accepted in October, 1988, toward a more "radical" attitude first had been perceptible in the Front's rural organizations, whose localities were predominantly Latvian. However, the central, executive bodies of the Popular Front were also moving toward the aim of independence. The Baltic Assembly, which is formed by all three republics' popular movements, declared in its meeting in Tallinn on May 13 and 14, in effect, for independence.

Why a shift to independence as the Front's main goal? A number of factors had contributed. There was disappointment about *perestroika*, a growing comprehension that it would not work. The Popular Front had discovered that dealing with Moscow was frustrating and futile. There was an upward flow of nationalist feeling from the Latvian population. And in Estonia and Lithuania, the two parallel organizations had been decisive in advancing political claims. Moreover, the effect of the work carried out by the Latvian National Independence Movement should not go unobserved.

The question was: how would the "old authority" respond to a Baltic declaration of independence? The executors of Moscow's will were the local Party and the Interfront. But neither one could react immediately or very effectively. The Latvian Communist Party had been weakened by internal divisions, while the Interfront was not as massive or united as it professed to be. Essentially, it was made up of the old, Brezhnevite party apparatus together with retired military—a group almost exclusively Russian by nationality and chauvinistic in outlook. However, it would be misleading to suggest that all Russian immigrants in Latvia were chauvinists. The Interfront had attempted to gather a mass following but had not been successful. Therefore, a declaration of independence would not necessarily be opposed immediately and unanimously by the non-Latvian part of the population.

Latvia was a multinational country. In the long run, a solution to the nationalities problem was a part of the solution to independence. Latvia in its former independent state offered a good example for study. More than one-fourth of the population of the independent republic had been non-Latvian and had enjoyed wide cultural autonomy. Today, many of the smaller ethnic groups (Jews, Poles) supported the Popular Front, whose policy was to reestablish cultural autonomy. Obviously, circumstances had changed since Latvia was independent. Some legislation was required on citizenship, on franchise and on Latvian as the state language. For instance, voting rights could not be granted immediately to all immigrants without considering length of residence, as the Interfront demanded for all Soviet Army soldiers (some recently arrived from distant republics) in local elections. Neither the United States nor any European state granted the right to vote upon demand, Mr. Berklavs pointed out. Those who wanted to be citizens should be able to speak some Latvian and have a certain length of residence. When independence became an issue to be dealt with directly—and such a time would soon come—the Popular Front and other organizations shared the task of explaining that these were reasonable requirements and not prejudicial to non-Latvian groups in the republic. A resolution of the nationalities question along the lines of cultural autonomy offered a good solution.

Mr. Badzo then spoke. A philologist by training, he was one of the prominent literati who had had a major role in the national and cultural revival in Ukraine that was brutally put down in 1972. Imprisoned in 1979, he was released only when *glasnost* was inaugurated.

Geographers, Mr. Badzo said, placed the center of Europe in Ukraine, but unfortunately not everyone was able to find it on the map of politics. This was a regrettable omission from Europe's outlook on history. The Baltic states were leaders in the democratization movement in the Soviet Union today and were rightly the center of attention of Western observers. But Ukraine's potential in the realms of politics, economics and culture was understood by those who had studied the nationality question in the Soviet empire.

There now had been years of change in the Soviet Union, but change had had the least visible effect in Belorussia and in Ukraine. The policy of Ukrainian First Secretary Shcherbitsky, who had come into office at a time when Brezhnev was trying to suppress Ukrainian nationalism, was very much in effect today. Ukraine's Party apparatus assiduously and very deliberately continued to carry out the old policies, constantly attacking all manifestations of the popular movement and doing all it could to put brakes on the national revival. The Kremlin knew this quite well and evidently approved.

Under such conditions, the most immediate and critically contested issues were language and culture. However, alongside demands for cultural and language rights, there was an increasing political content in the popular movement. Mr. Badzo himself belonged to the group that had proclaimed Ukraine's final aim to be political independence. Today, this demand definitely was picking up a wide following. Realistically assessing the current situation in Ukraine, Mr. Badzo felt independence could be reached.

For Rukh, the first factor to be considered was the scope of the movement itself. In August, 1989, before Rukh's congress had assembled, documents had reached the initiative group demonstrating that 250,000 persons had joined the movement. This was a considerable number. Furthermore, the rate of new members joining was accelerating. The second factor was the social composition of the organization, which embraced various levels of society and included numbers of organizations. This was very advantageous. The democratic and patriotic movement was being supported by an underlying network of organizations, informal associations and publications. Rukh was being built not only with individual members but on hierarchical tiers of organizations. The third factor was support from the outside, from the Baltic Popular Fronts. As early as 1988, representatives from Estonian, Latvian and Lithuanian groups (and from other republics' groups as well) had established a Coordinating Committee of the Patriotic Movement of the Peoples of USSR in Lvov. Subsequently, Ukrainians were invited to a meeting in Riga. There had been other meetings. When Rukh was initiated, one of its founders, Pavlo Movchan, acknowledged that the programs of the Baltic Popular Fronts provided a model for the Ukrainians.

In sum: all these factors had made for a large, integrated movement that no longer lived in isolation. The Ukrainians had outside allies, and they moved forward as a sector of a broad front.

The panel participants were asked to consider a theme suggested by Mr. Badzo. The Popular Fronts had arisen as a Baltic phenomenon. On their home ground, they had traveled faster and achieved more than similar movements in other republics. The Balts would argue that their success had much to do with their unique historical heritage, and there was much substance to this claim. But external considerations had to be taken into account, and matters could be viewed from other perspectives. One such could be called the "Moscow perspective." Simply put, it meant that small nations could ask for more than large ones. Moscow might not feel as threatened by the Baltic movements as by similar ones in, for example, Uzbekistan or Ukraine. Moscow's responses also seemed to be triggered by the size of a movement: witness its response to the huge but peaceful Baltic demonstration of August 23, 1989. Assuming that mass movements continued to move toward independence, which was a reasonable assumption to make, how would Moscow respond? And how would the representatives of the movements view future developments in their countries?

In viewing Estonia's experience, Ms. Lauristin said the interaction between the body and head of a popular movement, between the mass and its intellectual leadership, was a crucial requirement and an inevitable condition for the movement's success. In the case of some popular movements outside the Baltic, the organizations' rapid growth in size had outstripped the ability of the leadership, which included only a small number of intellectuals and professionals. Populist movements must be provided with programs, prospects and plans. Today this task fell to the intelligentsia. A particular Baltic characteristic was that there was no gap between the intellectuals and other social groups. The Popular Fronts had to operate with complicated and detailed legal and economic proposals on republican sovereignty and on economic models. However, within a few days of being issued, these had become matters of public discourse. Listening to what the public, the mass, had to say about the proposals gave information to the leadership on how to reassess and revise them. This proximity, a reciprocal flow of ideas, made the Baltic Popular Fronts very effective.

The popular movements in the Soviet Union faced an external danger from the old administrative and bureaucratic apparatus—a danger recognized by all. There also was an internal danger that the mass following could move away from well-considered programs, seize upon some peculiar proposal or career off on a course of its own. In Russia, there was the beginning of a popular movement, but there were groups with odd proposals: there were "neo-Bolsheviks," for instance. This did not necessarily mean that any popular movement in Russia would be seized by such a group. But a possibility always was there. In Azerbaijan, the mass movement had diverged greatly from its initial purpose of building a Popular Front and had entered into a violent national conflict.

Addressing Latvia's case, Mr. Berklavs first considered the immediate activities of the Latvian National Independence Movement, whose clear aim was mass support for Latvia's independence. The Movement had entered the recent All-Union elections (not as a rival of the Popular Front, since the Independence Movement belonged to the Front), running its own candidates on the issue and finding broad support. The support had been so pronounced that the rank and file of the Popular Front was now pushing the leadership of the organization toward declaring independence as its main political aim. The upcoming republic elections to local Soviets and the Supreme Soviet of Latvian SSR were also an opportunity. A majority of deputies could win mandates on the issue of independence. Thereby the demand for independence would be raised in a political forum that considered itself a parliamentary body. Adding to this push for independence were the Citizens' Committees, which together possibly contained more members than the Popular Front. They intended to convoke congresses that could claim legitimacy, as successors to the parliaments of the independent republics.

On the one hand, observers found the jostling between various movements, large and small, to be confusing. But an essential fact was that all of these movements had declared for independence, had popular support and were finding public forums and electoral offices to pursue their policies. It was one matter for Moscow to arrest a group of dissidents, another to suppress a movement of hundreds of thousands. The political landscape of the Baltic states had changed greatly, and the Communist Party was lost in it. The popular movements, on the other hand, were moving through it with much skill. Finally, the Latvians had been quite successful in presenting their case to the West and receiving public attention and support. All these efforts had created and consolidated new political positions in the Baltic.

Would Moscow make a strong move to overwhelm these positions held by Baltic separatists? One could envisage a variety of responses, including economic sanctions. The real danger lay in the use of large-scale military force. Its deployment could not be ruled out entirely, but four considerations argued against it. First, the popular movements had spread beyond the Baltic republics. If one republic were to be attacked, all others would respond. They would be permanently antagonized and always on the alert, maintaining defensive and hostile attitudes toward Moscow. And the Communist Party had never underestimated the potential of mass national opposition. Second, the republics' Communist parties were relatively weak, at least in the Baltic. They were internally divided, and there was no political arm that would execute Moscow's orders. Third, suppressing the Baltic movements would mean disrupting economic functions in the Baltic area. With the Soviet Union in a perilous economic situation, Gorbachev would think twice before risking foreign and domestic economic repercussions. There could be Western retaliation, with grave consequences for *perestroika*. Lastly, Western public opinion, the Western press and the policies of Western governments had to be considered. Taking into account all of these factors weighing against an aggressive response from Moscow, the Baltic movements could proceed toward independence, but this had to be done carefully, with the movements testing the ground in advance and not making abrupt moves that could elicit an instinctive response from the central authorities.

Mr. Badzo spoke of a broad gap in Ukraine separating the population from the Party-*cum*-state authority. The old Party clique's assault upon the popular movement was not abating. In a way, the inflexible, reactionary policies of the First Secretary had helped the opposition. The Party simply would not engage in reform, while the popular movement, which Mr. Badzo believed had a sufficient number of skilled people of a high intellectual caliber, had come up with a program proposing solutions to a broad range of social problems, encouraging other nationalities in the republic to join the movement. In sum, the Party's wholesale assault was consolidating disparate groups. The movement, Mr. Badzo added, was becoming bolder; demonstrations with 10,000 participants or more were becoming commonplace. For all of that, the situation in Ukraine was difficult and the attack from the Communist Party unremitting and vicious. As in the Baltic, the reactionary forces were attempting to exploit national rivalries and Russian chauvinism in fighting the reformers. Western press coverage, which had assisted the Baltic movements greatly, would also be of much help in Ukraine.

A question was then posed about the phenomenon of nationalism and a Communist's dilemma in dealing with it. According to Marxist-Leninist belief, national passions, national identities and national struggles belong to the "bourgeois-capitalist" stage of history. Socialism was supposed to have eliminated all national conflicts, because national feelings were no longer supposed to exist. Yet the Communist Party now was engulfed by an enormous nationality problem, very much of the same nature as the ones that rocked the empires of the 19th century. Did this issue ever arise when the leaders of the popular movements met the representatives of the Communist parties to discuss the present state of affairs? Did the Communists attempt to explain the collapse of their faith?

Responding to the question, Mr. Berklavs replied that the Communists avoided exploring their dilemma along such broad and theoretical lines. Instead, the problem was disguised by relegating all evils to the Stalinist period. However, the Party's practice of exploiting the nationality question in tactical political issues was unfortunately very much alive. He would describe this stance by detailing the deeds of Ivars Kezbers, ideological secretary of the Latvian Communist Party.

Mr. Kezbers had served the Soviet Union abroad, being posted to its embassy in Stockholm, from which position he was withdrawn with unseemly haste, possibly for engaging in matters beyond the normal concerns of diplomacy. Mr. Kezbers then had been in Moscow with the state radio. Afterwards, he was made the ideological secretary of the Latvian Communist Party. Here clearly was a man capable of dealing with the nationality question—someone with experience in the West, with experience as a propagandist in Moscow, and with ideological expertise. Yet Mr. Kezbers never made any pronouncements on the forces of nationalism today. Like all other Communists, he said that national emotions or conflicts were rooted in Stalinist distortions the Party had put decisively behind it. All evils had died with Stalin, and the Party was chaste, innocent and Leninist. In practice, however, the Party, which had had decades of experience in fostering national animosities for its own purposes, had deliberately and repeatedly introduced conflict between national groups. The uneasiness of the Russian population in the Baltic, the emergence of the interfronts: these events and others had all too frequently the Party's surreptitious and skilled hand behind them. This was how Communists dealt with the nationality issue—not by pondering where Marxist-Leninist theory went off the road.

All panel participants were then asked if they could envisage a time in the future when Moscow would decide to recognize a special status for the Baltic republics. According to this scenario, the Baltic states would be different from the other republics; they would be further removed from the center, and their status would be analogous to the one Finland enjoyed in the 19th century. Though a part of tsarist Russia, Finland had possessed real autonomy, a domestic administration with effective political power and a border that had definite significance. Assuming, further, that such an offer came from Moscow, how would the Baltic popular movements respond to it? Would they see it as an option to be considered?

Ms. Lauristin said she believed that a proposal similar to the one described had been included in the draft for a new program for the Estonian Communist Party. The Lithuanian Communist Party was considering similar plans. As to the Latvian Communists, they had not as yet worked out the draft for a new Party platform, but it was highly likely such points would be included. So the local parties, if not Moscow, wanted the historical status of Finland. On this issue, the Popular Fronts and a certain sector within the Communist parties could find common political ground.

However, the parties saw the "Finland status" as their final goal; for the Popular Fronts, it could be merely an intermediate or transitional stage before reaching independence.

Mr. Berklavs thought it was entirely conceivable that Moscow would come up with an offer along these lines. But an offer was one thing, and the current political reality was another. The Baltic states would have to scrutinize such approaches carefully to see what, if anything, they held out. There were plenty of reasons to be pessimistic about Moscow's approaches, even if such offers were accompanied by constitutional guarantees. Such guarantees existed today: Soviet constitutions were replete with them. So it all came down to credibility, and Moscow had no credibility in the eyes of the Baltic nations. Its offers simply would never be accepted at face value. One could theorize about federations or confederations, but at bottom the issue was who had power. And Moscow possessed power today. As long as the Baltic states were within the embrace of that power, they would never regain anything of political independence, civil liberties or economic recovery.

Second, the political and national conditions in each of the three Baltic republics was different, and the decision as to whether to accept such autonomous or intermediate stages had to be based on these conditions. The situation in Latvia, for example, differed greatly from the one in Lithuania. Today, as a result of deliberate Soviet policy, the Latvians constituted slightly over half of Latvia's population. If they were to continue to exist as a nation, they would have to move outside the Soviet Union and Soviet policy immediately. There was no time left for them. They could not wait 20 years, or even ten, in any in-between, provisional or autonomous status. Their circumstances compelled the Latvians to move toward independence as rapidly as possible. Some Western analysts said that the Baltic states had a role to play in accelerating *perestroika* and that without them *perestroika* would fail. The Baltic nations found such opinions peculiar: 50 years ago they had been forcefully imprisoned in the Soviet empire, and now, as the prison was collapsing, they were being asked by outsiders to repair it so neither they nor any other nation could escape. In any event, the Soviet Union was beyond help; no *perestroika* could salvage its collapsing economic structure. Either the Baltic peoples escaped from the structure or they would expire, as prisoners, within it.

The question under consideration pertained directly to the Baltic states, Mr. Badzo noted, but he would make some comment on Ukraine, whose national and political consciousness reached further than some outside observers thought. In the West, there was a general perception of a politically alert Western Ukraine, which was contrasted with a passive, russified Eastern Ukraine. But there were cases of Ukrainians who no longer spoke their language yet nonetheless supported the idea of independence. Historically, Russian and Ukrainian relations had been so negative that Ukrainians would not be able to affirm their rights of culture and language without splitting away from the Russians—and from the Soviet Union. Shcherbitsky's policy had certainly exacerbated this feeling. And this all pointed to separatism, Ukrainian statehood and true independence.

A question was posed about the sometimes confusing political terminology used by the Popular Fronts—such words as "federation," "confederation," "sovereignty" and "independence." The popular movement leaders were asked to define the meaning of these words. "Federation," for example, seemed completely inappropriate in describing the existing structure of the Soviet Union. How would the representatives of the Fronts envisage "federation," how would it differ from "confederation," and how did "sovereignty" differ from "independence"?

Ms. Lauristin explained that "federation," as used in common parlance, was what existed in the Soviet Union today, and, rightly or wrongly, the term would remain in popular usage. As for "confederation," a good example would be the relationship between Finland and imperial Russia in the 19th century. Such a "confederate" relationship would be greatly preferable to the present state of affairs. If a state had a confederate status of this kind, it could be said to enjoy "sovereignty." However, from the viewpoint of what could be achieved today, a confederation would be a temporary, or intermediate, period before reaching independence. An independent state would possess all powers over its domestic and foreign affairs.

Mr. Berklavs noted that in principle the distinctions should be clear, but much confusion had arisen in recent practice. Some of the confusion had been introduced deliberately as an obfuscation. "Independence" was a clear and precise term. It meant putting Latvia (or Estonia or Lithuania) outside the Soviet borders, definitely and permanently. "Republican sovereignty" was a broad, even loose, term that meant something short of independence. Individuals who now claimed to be for it ranged from people who would have Latvia one step short of independence to those who wanted minimal changes. "Confederation" was a term used by Moscow. It implied that Baltic demands for republican sovereignty could be accommodated within a new structure, a sort of confederation. What this confederation would offer had not yet been clearly stated; probably it would provide a degree of local autonomy, little more. It would be best if crucial political terminology were used according to well-established norms, particularly where rights of nations and national self-determination were at stake. But a lack of clarity, sometimes inadvertently, sometimes deliberately, had entered Baltic political dialogue.

The panel representatives were reminded that soon the CPSU Central Committee plenum on nationalities would take place. The draft program of the Party had already been published, so we already knew how the central leadership was thinking on this issue. How would the representatives of the popular movements regard the Party's decisions in Moscow?

Ms. Lauristin said that, to a degree, the Central Committee no longer was greatly relevant. There had been a decline in the Party's role in making central decisions of general validity or force. Nonetheless, the outcome of the plenum would be important, because it would indicate the true situation in the Soviet Union. We had, on the one hand, a relatively mild or reformist draft by Moscow's traditional standards. On the other hand, we had witnessed the rise of popular movements in Ukraine and other republics that distinctly threatened republic-level Party organizations and we also had witnessed the Central Committee's recent attack on the Baltic Popular Fronts. What would come from the plenum itself would be a political solution, harsher in terms than the preliminary draft.

The moderator, Toomas Ilves, thought that an outside observer might conclude that the preliminary document had been drafted some three years ago. From the Baltic viewpoint, it would be absurd to take the draft's theses completely seriously. For instance, the Baltic movements, much more than Moscow, were staking their future on representative bodies, even if these were still pseudo-parliamentary, and the importance of the local Communist parties was decreasing. While the Central Committee believed its decisions would be obeyed, the popular movements had gathered conviction in their own strength, in pursuing democracy and in giving political power to the local Supreme Soviets. Why should the Popular Fronts revert to accepting the old, traditional, behind-the-scenes decision making in Moscow?

Mr. Berklavs noted that the Central Committee plenum had been in the making for more than a year and had been repeatedly postponed. Its agenda had been shaped by intervening events, and its outcome would be even more distinctly determined by such events. Actually, the broad developments today could not be viewed as one kind of nationalism and placed under the same heading of nationalism without any differentiation. First, we had conflicts among nationalities, as, for example, in Armenia. To such events the Central Committee would attempt to give an answer. The second set of events was the expansion of the popular movements in the Baltic republics. These movements would trouble the Party much more, because the central issue they presented was the principle of national self-determination. This principle the Party plenum would circumvent and avoid. It simply was not acceptable to the Party's dogma: self-determination did not deal, at bottom, with restructuring the Soviet state along the lines of altering the federation. It dealt with the Soviet Union as an empire. What one could expect from the plenum were minimal concessions made to the popular movements, as attempts to conceal or disguise the real issues. But once the central power, the Central Committee, was incited into making its true opinion revealed, as it had been on August 26, it showed an unyielding, intransigent opposition to national demands.

Mr. Badzo stated that the Party's platform would be of importance chiefly as an object of study, which would reveal its inability to comprehend the national question. The draft platform simply showed the continuity of old thinking. For instance, it did not envisage granting cultural autonomy to the republics. Such issues remained under Moscow's central control. The document even attempted to resuscitate the old, Brezhnevite concept of a "Soviet people" (*sovetskii narod*). As to the fundamental issue, the structure of the state, the Party was entirely reluctant to envisage any decentralization, any movement toward confederation. Nor was any decentralization envisaged for the Party apparatus. If one were to view the draft platform and the plenum as a preamble or introduction to anything, Mr. Badzo concluded, it would be an introduction to division, to the more rapid growth of the national movements and to their increasing radicalization.

PART THREE

The Counterforce

5

The Party and Popular Movements in the Baltic

Kestutis Girnius

The struggle for power and influence in the Baltic republics is not only a duel between the local Communist Party and popular movement. Recent events have served as a reminder that at least two other groups have a singular role in determining events: the central authorities in Moscow and the masses below, either the native Baltic populations or those described rather uncharitably as migrants. None of the groups has had a consistent part or been implementing patiently a coherent strategy. Moscow's current threatening posture should not obscure the fact that in the summer of 1988 it protected Sajudis from possible repression by the Lithuanian Communist Party and was responsible for appointing relatively liberal First Secretaries in all three Baltic states. The local Party leadership has had to assess constantly how its decisions would be received in Moscow and also monitor the comings and goings of special commissions and emissaries.[1]

Both the Communist parties and the popular movements have had to adjust their preferred policy to take into account three elements: the progressively more radical demands from below, Moscow's growing disenchantment and the need somehow to cap the revolution of rising expectations. Pressure from below is growing, threats from Moscow have increased, the longing for independence is attaining a critical mass. Appeals to realism, uttered publicly by leading Party figures and no less urgently in the councils of the popular movements, have diminishing returns. Much that seemed completely beyond the pale has taken place:

---

[1] Background for Lithuanian developments is given in V. Stanley Vardys, "Lithuanian National Politics," *Problems of Communism*, XXXVIII (July–August, 1989), 53–76.

the restoration of national symbols, the emergence of a multiparty system, the resurrection of civil society, public condemnation of the occupation of 1940, vociferous calls for the withdrawal of the Red Army and serious discussion of the revival of Party independence. The radicals have become increasingly convinced that the steady escalation of pressure will ensure further concessions. Momentum is on their side.[2]

Moscow's lack of a coherent nationalities policy has undermined the authority of those who have tried to draw a firm line between what is permissible and what is not. In the early stages, the Kremlin clearly favored reform, but it fumbled badly when it faced its first major challenge— the Estonian declaration of sovereignty in November, 1988. Gorbachev's contradictory statements and the failure to enforce the decision of the Supreme Soviet of the USSR declaring the Estonian declaration null and void were costly. The radicalization of word and deed has proceeded, threatening to sweep aside not only the local Party leadership but also the governing bodies of the popular movements. Sajudis's parliamentary council has been frequently criticized by leading activists, particularly from Kaunas, for being too conciliatory.[3] The Estonian and Latvian Popular Fronts have become more radical in response to the challenge of, for example, the Latvian Independence Party and the Citizens' Committees.

The percentage of the non-indigenous population is an important variable determining Party and movement policy. Because of the relatively favorable demographic situation in Lithuania, the local Party and Sajudis could fight for influence without too much worry about the reaction of non-Lithuanians. In Estonia, the unfavorable demographic situation and perceived threat to national existence was a significant factor in the early emergence of the Popular Front, the favorable response of the Party and the relative unity of purpose that has since prevailed. This unity of purpose in turn helps explain the militancy of Estonia's Intermovement, whose activists see the leadership of the Estonian Communist Party as hostile to their aspirations of maintaining Soviet control over the republic. The

---

[2] See Saulius Girnius, "The 'Lithuanian Restructuring Movement,'" *Radio Free Europe Research*, August 4, 1988; Kestutis Girnius, "Three Months of Change in Lithuania," *Radio Free Europe Research*, August 31, 1988; and Kestutis Girnius, "Lithuanian Dissent: Proud Past, Uncertain Future," *Radio Free Europe Research*, October 5, 1988.

[3] For these divided opinions, see *Atgimimas*, November 22 and November 29, 1988. Concerning Latvia, see Dzintra Bungs, "New Group for Latvian Independence Formed," *Radio Free Europe Research*, July 13, 1988. For Estonia, see Toomas Ilves, "Radical Resolutions Adopted by Meeting of Official and Unofficial Youth Groups," *Radio Free Europe Research*, July 13, 1988.

Latvian Party's reluctance to embrace more radical demands may be attributable to the fact that non-Latvians constitute a sizable majority of Party members.[4]

In analyzing the relationship of movement and Party in Lithuania, a relationship that has been more dynamic than in Latvia and Estonia, four distinct phases are readily identifiable. In the first phase, lasting from June to October, 1988, the leadership of the Party viewed Sajudis with undisguised enmity. The second phase, a honeymoon lasting but a month and a half, ended when Sajudis vehemently protested against the manipulations that led to the decision by the Lithuanian Supreme Soviet to reject a declaration of sovereignty. The third phase was one of open political competition that ended with the Party's crushing defeat in the March, 1989, elections. This ushered in the fourth phase, in which the Party has adopted many Sajudis positions and attempted to distance itself from Moscow, creating the impression that it is an independent patriotic force that deserves to be considered the senior partner.[5]

One factor has remained constant through all four phases. Burdened by its unpopular past and tied by loyalty to Moscow, the Lithuanian Party consistently has been in the awkward situation of trying to bridge the gap between its position and the national mood. Even its most daring plans are always too little too late—faint echoes of more imaginative Sajudis proposals. For example, the discussion concerning plans to create an independent Lithuanian Communist Party seems parochial when Sajudis is calling for national independence.

Although many factors have contributed to the rise of Sajudis to unprecedented influence—influence greater than that achieved by the Popular Fronts in Estonia and Latvia—the Party's frequently inept responses must be taken into account. The deeply conservative and unimaginative leadership of the Lithuanian Communist Party, among whom bureaucrats of the Brezhnev mold were legion, failed to gauge the public mood in the euphoric days of the summer of 1988, believing that it could weather the storm with minimal concessions.[6] This belief was mistaken. Within two months, Sajudis spokesmen, rather than those of the Central Committee, were setting the agenda for Lithuanian public life. The Party's policy of vacillation pleased neither reformers nor hard-liners. Most importantly,

---

    [4] See Juris Dreifelds, "Latvian National Rebirth," *Problems of Communism*, XXXVIII (July–August, 1989), 77–95; and Rein Taagepera, "Estonia in September 1988: Stalinists, Centrists and Restorationists," *Journal of Baltic Studies*, XX (Summer, 1989), 175–190.

    [5] Vardys, "Lithuanian National Politics," 60–61.

    [6] Kestutis Girnius, "First Secretary Songaila on the Restructuring and Other Current Problems," *Radio Free Europe Research*, October 28, 1988.

the Party was becoming increasingly isolated from the populace. A visit by Soviet Communist Party Central Committee Secretary Aleksandr Yakovlev in August, 1988, forced the Party to moderate its policy toward Sajudis and the national renewal. The Party also was forced to accept the national symbols of independent Lithuania (its flag and coat of arms), the official status of the Lithuanian language and the rewriting of history texts. The credit gained by these measures was squandered when force was used to disperse demonstrators on September 28, 1988.

The Party received a second chance when Algirdas Brazauskas was appointed First Secretary two days before the constituent congress of Sajudis was convened in Vilnius on October 22, 1988.[7] Brazauskas made a number of astute political moves that augmented his popularity, the decision to return Vilnius's cathedral to the Catholic church being the most spectacular. Party and Sajudis leaders began coordinating their activities, as, for example, in the campaign protesting proposed changes to the USSR Constitution that would have limited the rights of the Union republics.[8] The spirit of conciliation soon fell victim to the dictates of political reality, to rising expectations and to Gorbachev's clumsy intervention. Ordered to prevent the passage of a declaration of sovereignty similar to that adopted in Estonia several days earlier, Brazauskas used his prestige and influence, as well as some questionable procedural maneuvers, to block discussion of the proposed amendment in Lithuania's Supreme Soviet.[9] Sajudis reacted with dismay, particularly because Brazauskas was the Party leader they had wanted to trust. The honeymoon was over. The Party and Sajudis were once again on different sides of the barricades.

This parting of ways had far-reaching consequences. Brazauskas's obeisance to Moscow was the most decisive event of the year. It must be remembered that, despite Lithuanians' disenchantment and often disgust with Party rule, its very longevity created an aura of irrevocability. It held all the perquisites and levers of power as well as the blessing of the Kremlin, at that time a sine qua non for all serious pretenders to rule. In Brazauskas, the Party had a leader who could satisfy the need of many to believe in the virtue of the man at the top, one who seemed capable of rallying to the Party's standard the many Communists in the Sajudis leadership still unprepared to sever ties with the Party. The Lithuanian Communist Party

---

[7] Saulius Girnius, "A New Party First Secretary: Algirdas Brazauskas," *Radio Free Europe Research*, October 28, 1988.

[8] Saulius Girnius, "Growing Dissatisfaction with Proposed Changes to the Soviet Constitution," *Radio Free Europe Research*, November 22, 1988.

[9] Saulius Girnius, "The Latest Session of the Lithuanian Supreme Soviet," *Radio Free Europe Research*, November 22, 1988.

could coopt the revolution from below, moderate the demands of Sajudis by strengthening the influence of the so-called realists, perhaps even provoke a split between Sajudis radicals and moderates.[10] Brazauskas's refusal to support the sovereignty declaration changed all that. Stung by the Party's action, Sajudis decided to buttress its independent standing and challenge the Party by fielding a full slate of candidates in the elections to the Congress of People's Deputies in March. The nation was to be given a clear choice between Sajudis and the Party.[11] With the Party once again discredited, radical sentiments gained the upper hand. Within four months, Sajudis's parliament had issued a call for national independence.

As the elections approached, it was evident that defeat loomed for the Party, which then resorted to traditional carrot and stick tactics. At the so-called "black plenum" of February 21, Party conservatives launched a bitter tirade against Sajudis, while Brazauskas warned that Lithuania was but a step away from the imposition of a "special form of rule," threatening the republic with the fate of Armenians in Nagorno-Karabakh.[12] Yet the time for intimidation was past. The plenum evoked more anger than fear.

Realizing the attractiveness of Sajudis's program, the Party made a major effort to follow its example by appealing to national and patriotic sentiments. The Party placed unprecedented emphasis on maximum national sovereignty for Lithuania within the USSR, proclaiming that a Lithuania without sovereignty was a Lithuania without a future. The strategy did not work. Sajudis candidates won 36 or 37 of the 42 races (depending on whether Sajudis can claim a victory in the one electoral district in which a locally supported Sajudis candidate defeated the candidate endorsed by Sajudis's parliamentary council).[13] The importance of the victory was immense. The Party could no longer pretend to speak for the nation. Sajudis was assured of its mandate and acted accordingly. Sajudis deputies dominated the Lithuanian delegation at the Congress of People's Deputies and made the important decisions. Brazauskas was not the delegation's chairman.

---

[10] On the Party's maneuvers, see *Tiesa*, December 17, 1988, and February 7, 1989; and Vardys, "Lithuanian National Politics," 67–68. On the Party and the Catholic church, see Kestutis Girnius, "Bishop Steponavicius Allowed to Resume His Duties," *Radio Free Europe Research*, January 5, 1989.

[11] *Atgimimas*, February 17, 1989; and Vardys, "Lithuanian National Politics," 69–70.

[12] *Tiesa*, February 23, 1989.

[13] Saulius Girnius, "The Elections for the USSR Congress of People's Deputies," *Radio Free Europe Research*, March 16, 1989; and Saulius Girnius, "Sajudis Candidates Sweep Elections," *Radio Free Europe Research*, April 21, 1989.

After the election debacle, the Lithuanian Communist Party made a great effort to match its program to the prevailing national mood, to set the pace rather than bring up the rear. On May 18, 1989, the Lithuanian Supreme Soviet passed the declaration of Lithuanian sovereignty and four amendments to the constitution, allocating to itself the right to determine whether All-Union laws would be implemented.[14] On June 24, the Party convened its 18th plenum to discuss the urgent need to redefine the status, program and regulations of the Communist Party. It was a revolutionary event. Many speakers called for the creation of an autonomous Party, pointing out that its continued subordination to the Communist Party of the Soviet Union (CPSU) was not in line with the striving for national sovereignty. Although Brazauskas spoke up for realism and emphasized the need to balance harmoniously the sovereignty of Lithuania with that of the USSR, other speakers were less restrained. The First Secretary of Kaunas's Party organization recommended that CPSU decisions be applicable only if approved by the Lithuanian Communist Party and urged that the plenum express its approval of a multiparty system. Others urged that the reference in the constitution to the leading role of the Party be eliminated and that the CPSU be changed into a union of republican parties, whose politburo would consist of a representative from each party. Although the plenum resolutions included a call to convene a special Party congress that year to discuss the Lithuanian Communist Party's future ties with the CPSU, the tenor of the resolutions was far more moderate than the speeches, suggesting that Brazauskas, with his ears attuned to Moscow's whispers and growls, was by no means the Party's greatest liberal.[15]

Nonetheless, Brazauskas's popularity remained great. A poll conducted on May 21–23, 1989, indicated that he received an 84 percent favorable rating, while the Party itself received a mere 22 percent;[16] at the end of August, Brazauskas's popularity was almost as high. Articles in the Lithuanian press suggest that a majority of Lithuania's Communists believe that the Lithuanian Communist Party should become an autonomous party, regulating its ties with the CPSU on the basis of treaties between equals. Some conservatives are of course opposed to such a solution, but there are also radicals within the Party who want to break completely with the past, and even change the Party's name to the Lithuanian Socialist or Social Justice Party. Support for the most radical solution grew steadily. According to the August, 1989, poll, 64 percent of Party members desired a sovereign Lithuanian Communist Party whose ties with the

---

[14] Saulius Girnius, "Lithuania Declares Its Sovereignty," *Radio Free Europe Research*, May 31, 1989.

[15] *Tiesa*, June 28 and July 5, 1989.

[16] Published in *Komjaunimo Tiesa*, June 16, 1989.

CPSU would be regulated by a treaty, 20 percent wanted greater autonomy within the CPSU, nine percent desired no changes and seven percent had no opinion.

If the case of the Lithuanian Komsomol is a guide, such measures will not be enough to regain the people's trust. In a stormy congress that was forced to adjourn for two weeks, the Lithuanian Komsomol decided to sever its ties with the All-Union Komsomol. It further declared the reestablishment of the Lithuanian Communist Youth League and adopted a statute stating that its goal was "to strive for and defend the sovereignty of the Lithuanian SSR on the basis of the welfare of its citizens [and] to create a democratic state." Nonetheless, leaders of other Lithuanian youth organizations roundly condemned the Komsomol for failure to reform itself.[17]

Deep change is in the offing, in part because it is absolutely necessary for the Party to take dramatic steps to refurbish its image and shed some of the opprobrium of the past when entering elections. Without a fundamental reorientation of its position, the Party will always be badly mauled. Although political exigency makes radical change mandatory, it is not the sole motivating force. Party members, particularly the intelligentsia, have demanded change. Many Sajudis activists retain feelings of loyalty to the Party of their youth and remain convinced that a radically altered Party still has a role to play in political life.

The prospects for the Party's rehabilitation are hardly encouraging. It has had difficulties both writing a credible program and finding suitable candidates to challenge Sajudis. An imitation of Sajudis's program would always be considered second best—an imperfect clone, so to speak. An attempt to be more amenable to Moscow's concerns would strengthen the Party's standing among some non-Lithuanians but further alienate it from the majority of the population. Ideological considerations rule out the remaining alternative—attempting to be more radical than Sajudis. Finding attractive candidates requires conjuring skills of the first order, for in March, 1989, even decent men suffered crushing defeat when they ran as Party candidates. Even if it does not do Moscow's bidding but aims for a compromise solution, many will see the Party's willingness to compromise as yet another sign of its lukewarm commitment to national independence. The central authorities have done much to damage the prestige of the Lithuanian Communist Party. If it were not for the looming shadow of the Kremlin, the Lithuanian Communist Party would now be a relatively insignificant opposition party.

The Party's main hope lies in forging a coalition between its most liberal wing and the Communist Sajudis leaders. The Party has appealed to the

---

[17] Saulius Girnius, "The Lithuanian Komsomol Congress," *Radio Free Europe Research*, August 11, 1989.

latter to accept Party positions and join the work of reconstruction from within, rather than yielding to fancy and hoping that the Kremlin will just let Lithuania go. If a sufficient number of Sajudis Communists were enticed by such a suggestion, the radicals might demand changes in the composition of the leading Sajudis organs, thus precipitating a split in the movement. Such a possibility existed during the summer of 1989. However, Moscow's recent attacks have lead to greater unity among Sajudis members.

In the past year, Yedinstvo, the Lithuanian interfront, has increased its activities. Russians from outside the republic are said to be agitating their fellow countrymen to fight Lithuanian separatism. Non-Lithuanians, mostly directors or responsible executives of major factories, have formed the Council of Party Secretaries, which intends to challenge the dominant policy line of the Lithuanian Communist Party. Such activities might evoke a Lithuanian backlash and lead to a polarization along roughly ethnic lines, an unfortunate development that could only benefit Moscow.[18]

Turning to Estonia, the most singular feature of the situation in the republic has been the early and relatively consistent support of the Party for radical reform and the national aspirations of the indigenous population. The national rebirth in Estonia began shortly before those of Latvia and Lithuania. On April 1 and 2, 1988, the leadership of the Estonian cultural unions adopted a resolution calling for radical change in the relationship between Moscow and Tallinn and the granting of greater autonomy to Estonia. The resolution also claimed the Estonian nation was in danger of extinction and castigated the republican leadership for its incompetence and unwillingness to defend the national cause.[19] Several weeks later, the Estonian Popular Front was founded primarily by reformist and patriotic Communist intellectuals. Adopting a program based on the resolutions of the cultural unions, the Popular Front won ready acceptance in a population angered by the indifference of the Party leadership and brooding about an impending demographic crisis.[20] Instead of ordering a crackdown, Moscow appointed Vaino Valjas as First Secretary on June 16, 1988.[21] Valjas, a former Estonian Communist Party ideological secretary who had been removed from his post in 1980 reportedly for failure to implement reaction-

---

[18] Concerning Yedinstvo, see *Tiesa*, November 11, 1988, and February 14, 1989; and *Sovetskaya Litva*, May 16, 1989.

[19] Toomas Ilves, "Cultural Unions Adopt Resolution on Nationality Reforms," *Radio Free Europe Research*, June 3, 1988.

[20] Toomas Ilves, "The People's Front: The Creation of a Quasi Political Party," *Radio Free Europe Research*, May 20, 1988.

[21] Toomas Ilves, "Party First Secretary Replaced by Native Estonian," *Radio Free Europe Research*, July 13, 1988.

ary policy, moved quickly to spruce up the Party's image and his own status as a reformer. He immediately endorsed some of the demands of the creative unions, and the rehabilitation of the Estonian tricolor gained popularity for him and Arnold Ruutel, the chairman of the presidium of the Estonian Supreme Soviet.[22]

At the beginning of June, several large demonstrations in Tallinn and Tartu clearly demonstrated both the depth of Estonian dissatisfaction with Party rule and the breadth of the growing opposition movement. Valjas's appointment and his conciliatory stance helped defuse what could have been an explosive situation. They also gave the Party a breathing space to regroup and to rethink its political activity. The time was not wasted. At the Party plenum of September 9, 1988, Valjas reversed the position of the Estonian Communist Party on most issues.[23] He expressed support for a strong language law, Estonian citizenship and Estonian sovereignty in matters other than defense and foreign policy, and spoke out against continued immigration of non-Estonians. In effect, he endorsed the views that were first enunciated by the radical nationalist intelligentsia and whose promulgation but a year before could have led to imprisonment. Valjas attended the constituent congress of the Popular Front, held on October 1 and 2. In his address to the congress delegates, he conveyed Gorbachev's blessing of their movement and stated that the Party and the Popular Front did not oppose each other. Nevertheless, he indicated that the Front should not try to gain a position parallel to that of the Party.

Two months later, Gorbachev may well have rued his blessing. On November 16, the Estonian Supreme Soviet, with Valjas presiding, adopted a declaration of sovereignty, allowing it to be the final arbiter of the validity of All-Union legislation in Estonia. The Estonian Communist Party did not back down when the presidium of the USSR Supreme Soviet declared the new law unconstitutional.[24] This stance consolidated the alliance between Party and Popular Front and to a somewhat lesser degree between the Party and the Estonian nation. With the Communists in effect adopting its platform, the Estonian Popular Front had little reason to oppose the Party. Relations between Party and Popular Front became quite amicable; Party leaders were rarely criticized and continued to dominate public life.

---

[22] Taagepera, "Estonia in September 1988," 188–190.

[23] Toomas Ilves, "The New First Secretary's New Agenda," *Radio Free Europe Research*, October 5, 1988.

[24] On the political conflict, see Vardys, "Lithuanian National Politics," 67–68; Dreifelds, "Latvian National Rebirth," 86–87; and Saulius Girnius, "Baltic Condemnation of Proposed Changes to Soviet Constitution," *Radio Free Europe Research*, November 17, 1988.

Because of this spirit of concord, the Estonian Popular Front failed to develop as sophisticated an organizational structure as Sajudis, and its regional branches published far fewer independent publications. The Estonian Popular Front did not field a full slate of candidates in the March, 1989, elections; in many electoral districts, it was content to express its preference for liberal Party members. The population at large seemed more skeptical of the Party's good will. According to a poll conducted in April, 50 percent of Estonians would vote for the Popular Front, and only seven percent for the Party.[25]

The similarity of views between Party leadership and Popular Front is not just a matter of personalities or philosophical affinity. Demography plays a vital role. Almost 40 percent of the population consists of non-Estonians, whose ethnic consciousness and sense of injustice are being galvanized gradually by the passage of language and citizenship laws as well as by the agitation of Intermovement. Ethnic loyalties are playing an ever more crucial role in determining political stances; support for the current reform program is now considered a pro-Estonian position, opposition to it a pro-Russian one. The growing hostility of some Russians and their expressed desire for a return to more orthodox rule has impressed on both Party and Popular Front the advantages of cooperation.[26] The Estonian Communist Party cannot risk a major confrontation with the Popular Front that would alienate Estonians. In turn, the Popular Front must seek a modus vivendi with the current Party leadership, because the most likely replacements for Valjas and his companions are liable to be far less sympathetic to the Estonian national cause. It is worth remembering that non-Estonians are said to make up more than 50 percent of the membership of the Estonian Communist Party, so the possibility of reaction cannot be underestimated.

Pressure from below in the form of the Estonian Citizens' Committee has created difficulties for the rather cozy relationship between the Estonian Communist Party and the Popular Front. The leadership of the Estonian Citizens' Committee, which was established in the spring of 1989 by three pro-independence organizations, believes that the Popular Front and the Party have been lax in advocating the cause of Estonian independence. The Committee has initiated the process of registering citizens of the former Estonian republic and their descendants, with the intention of convening a congress that would discuss the most important unresolved political issues in the republic. The Citizens' Committee and its congress

---

[25] Toomas Ilves, "Poll on Independence and Political Parties," *Radio Free Europe Research*, May 31, 1989.

[26] Vello Pettai, "Strikers Look to Moscow for Help," *Radio Free Europe Research*, September 11, 1989.

could become the focus of an alternative political structure that would challenge the legitimacy of current institutions that were established and developed by an occupying power.[27]

The Popular Front at first ignored the existence of the Citizens' Committee, in part because it foresaw a future rival, in part because it believed the question of independence was too sensitive to be raised at the time. Even after it was forced to recognize the Committee, the leadership of the Front did not join in the action to register citizens. Local Popular Front organizations, however, have taken a friendlier stance toward the Committee, and many have assisted in the registration drive. The Estonian Communist Party has been more aloof. Central Committee Secretary Miik Titma warned the organizers of the Committee of the possible dangerous consequences of their actions, without specifying what those dangers were.

If the Estonian Citizens' Committee begins to gather strength, the Popular Front will feel the need to adopt a more radical stance on independence to preserve its influence among the population. For ideological and other reasons, the Estonian Communist Party has less leeway to adjust its position. Were the Central Committee to express overt support for Estonian independence, many rank and file non-Estonian members might revolt and start clamoring for a change in leadership. What is more, Intermovement might be galvanized into a new series of protest actions, thus increasing political tension. Because the Front and the Party represent different constituencies, the rise of the Citizens' Committee may drive a wedge between the Party and the Front or, at least, cause them to adopt different stands on the central question of Estonian independence.

In Latvia, the Party's initial response to the national awakening was somewhat different than it was in Estonia. In 1987 and early 1988, the Party's reaction was a mixture of confusion and anger as well as an attempt to comprehend the change in public mood.[28] But no attempt was made to resort to force, and by June, 1988, First Secretary Boris Pugo had appropriated some of the key demands of the intellectuals, including the call for republican sovereignty, the control of emigration and the placing of limits on the central ministries' authority.[29] As in Lithuania, the advocates of more force-

---

[27] Vello Pettai, "Estonian Citizens' Committees To Organize Congress of Estonian Citizens," *Radio Free Europe Research*, July 7, 1989.

[28] Parts of the record of the proceedings of a Party Central Committee plenum in June 1988, which debated the situation in Latvia, were published in *Baltic Forum*, IV (Fall, 1988).

[29] Dreifelds, "Latvian National Rebirth," 89; and Dzintra Bungs, "The Latvian Communist Party Leadership's Platform," *Radio Free Europe Research*, July 13, 1988.

ful measures against what they considered the spread of nationalism and disorder were restrained by their fear that such action would be considered incompatible with *perestroika* and might evoke Gorbachev's wrath.

Moscow remained unsatisfied with the belated and grudging response of the Latvian Communist Party leadership to the national ferment. During his visit in August, 1988, Aleksandr Yakovlev sought to galvanize the Party into action by convincing it of the need to renounce its passive attitude toward the new developments and to take charge of the situation by embracing the new movements and giving them proper guidance.[30] On September 30, Boris Pugo was appointed chairman of the CPSU Central Committee Party Control Commission. Several days later, Janis Vagris, an uninspired choice, was chosen the new First Secretary.[31] Under Vagris's leadership, the Latvian Communist Party made a substantial number of personnel changes and announced plans to reduce the number of Party functionaries.

Although Vagris was an ideological conservative incapable of arousing enthusiastic support, the Kremlin had little choice but to select a man of his mold. A First Secretary who attempted to satisfy the national aspirations of ethnic Latvians or assuage their fears of future extinction would invariably be forced to favor measures that the non-Latvian majority of the Latvian Communist Party would find nationalistic and unacceptable. A First Secretary who managed not to offend the Party faithful would be anathema to Latvian patriots, who would consider him indifferent to the most pressing national problems. Vagris was the unhappy compromise who pleased neither side.

The appointments of Vagris in Latvia and Brazauskas in Lithuania illustrate Gorbachev's dilemma once the genie of national rebirth had been released. The local Party organization could retain influence only if its leadership hewed closely to the public mood. This required adopting an ever more independent course of action, leading to a proportionate decline in Moscow's influence. When the republican Party organization showed greater solicitude for the interests of the Kremlin and refrained from actions that emphasized its capacity for independent action, its local influence continued to decline. Thus, when Latvian Communists were asked in the summer of 1989 to name the party they thought to have the greatest influence, only 11 percent chose their own.

There is no single explanation for the relative indecisiveness of the Latvian Party and Popular Front, but Latvia's unfavorable demographic

---

[30] Dzintra Bungs, "Yakovlev in Latvia: An Exercise in 'Socialist Pluralism,'" *Radio Free Europe Research*, August 26, 1988.

[31] On the choice of Vagris, see *Christian Science Monitor*, March 7, 1989; and Dreifelds, "Latvian National Rebirth," 89.

situation must surely play an essential role. It is now widely believed that Latvians make up approximately half of Latvia's population and about 33 percent of the republican Communist Party membership. Latvians are a minority in the major cities, including the capital of Riga. Continued immigration and the low birth rate among Latvians preclude any sudden improvement in the Latvians' share of the population, while a further decline seems probable.[32]

Because they were a clear minority in the republican Party organization, Latvians had to tread very carefully in order to avoid antagonizing fellow Party members and drawing upon themselves the charge of nationalism. Supporters of greater autonomy from Moscow were aware that they could be outvoted in Party organizations if sensitive issues came to a vote. Latvia's exceptional demographic situation also contributed to making many of the leading cadres of the Latvian Communist Party more pro-Soviet than Party leaders in Tallinn and Vilnius. The Popular Front faced similar difficulties and had to adopt a more moderate and conciliatory tone to avoid antagonizing the great mass of non-Latvians residing in the republic. Much progress has been made in convincing these citizens not to view Latvian independence as a threat to their future. But much more work has to be done if Latvia is to embark on a successful effort to gain independence.

---

[32] Concerning the demographic situation in Latvia, see Juris Dreifelds, "Demographic Trends in Latvia," *Nationalities Papers*, XII (No. 1, 1984).

6

Reaction: The Intermovement in Estonia

Toomas Hendrik Ilves

In the face of rising nationalism in the border republics, a conservative movement has sprung up with the purpose of maintaining Soviet power in non-Russian areas.[1] Estonia's Interdvizhenie or Intermovement (from "internationalist movement") and its related organizations, the Interfront of Latvia and Moldavia and Yedinstvo (Unity) of Lithuania, are to a large extent acting jointly as domestic fifth columns to defend central control. Indeed Yedinstvo of Lithuania has a sister organization that calls itself "The Group for the Maintenance of Soviet Power." Most non-Russian republics as well as the RSFSR proper also have parallel organizations with identical platforms bearing names that are variations of the designation "The United Council of Production Collectives." In some republics, most conspicuously in Moldavia and Estonia, such organizations and the interfronts share virtually identical directorates. Thus far the "inters" have been most active in Estonia, but what can be said of them there can be said about other areas where they have cropped up.

The national movement in Estonia began in the spring of 1987. It came first as an eruption of protest against russification after Moscow announced plans to create phosphate mines in Estonia,[2] an economic development that would have brought massive numbers of non-Estonians to an already over-

---

[1] For the background of Estonia's political circumstances and the emergence of Intermovement, see Rein Taagepera, "Estonia in September 1988: Stalinists, Centrists and Restorationists," *Journal of Baltic Studies*, XX (Summer, 1989), 175–190. For Estonia during Brezhnev's rule, see T. Parming and E. Jarvesoo, eds., *A Case Study of a Soviet Republic: The Estonian SSR* (Boulder, Co.: Westview, 1978).

[2] Mare Taagepera, "The Ecological and Political Problems of Phosphate Mining in Estonia," *Journal of Baltic Studies*, XX (Summer, 1989), 165–174.

burdened country. Protest took on an overt political tone when, in August, 1987, former political prisoners organized a memorial protesting the Nazi-Soviet Pact of 1939, in which Molotov and Ribbentrop partitioned the Baltic.[3] In the spring of 1988, in a joint plenum of creative unions, the intelligentsia revolted against the policies of Estonian Communist Party First Secretary Karl Vaino. The plenum's resolutions stated a number of demands, notably related to ecology, and issued a call for republican sovereignty.[4]

The demands of the plenum were adopted and expanded by the Popular Front, a grass-roots movement that began pushing for reforms within the system as well as championing a number of nationally minded innovations. In June, 1988, Karl Vaino fell and was replaced by Vaino Valjas, who in turn adopted much of the Popular Front program at the Estonian Communist Party plenum of September, 1988.[5]

The Intermovement was born in the summer of 1988 amid a resurgent Estonian national awareness symbolized by the rehabilitation of the flag of independent Estonia, the blue-black-white tricolor. First making its presence known two months after the appearance of the Popular Front, Intermovement held its formal founding congress on March 14, 1989. By this time Estonia's Supreme Court had passed laws establishing republican sovereignty and making Estonian the republic's official language. Intermovement had opposed the language decision and the flag of independent Estonia from the outset. At its founding congress, which was accompanied by a demonstration with some 30,000 to 40,000 participants, Intermovement listed among its demands the repeal of language laws and the outlawing of independent Estonia's flag, voiced its opposition to territorial economic management (or *khozraschet*), insisted that the Estonian Communist Party's top leadership be removed from office as "nationalistic" and on top of everything demanded that the heavily russified northeastern part of Estonia, along with Tallinn, the republic's capital, be annexed to the Leningrad oblast of the RSFSR. At least one speaker at the congress demanded mass deportations of Estonians.[6]

---

[3] On this and a subsequent demonstration in the following year, see Toomas Ilves, "Demonstration on the 49th Anniversary of the Molotov-Ribbentrop Pact," *Radio Free Europe Research*, August 26, 1989.

[4] Toomas Ilves, "Protest Letter from Leaders of Cultural Unions," *Radio Free Europe Research*, January 21, 1988; Toomas Ilves, "Unprecedented Openness at Cultural Unions' Plenum," *Radio Free Europe Research*, June 3, 1988; Toomas Ilves, "The Cultural Unions' Resolution to the Leaderships of the ECP and ESSR," *ibid.*

[5] Toomas Ilves, "Party First Secretary Replaced by Native Estonian," *Radio Free Europe Research*, July 13, 1988; Toomas Ilves, "The New First Secretary," *ibid.*, October 5, 1988.

[6] Radio Tallinn broadcast, March 14, 1989.

Tensions increased throughout the spring of 1989. Five Intermovement members were elected to the All-Union Congress of Deputies. Yevgeny Kogon, the movement's de facto leader, emerged as the most vociferous opponent of Estonian *khozraschet* in the Supreme Soviet of the Soviet Union. When Estonia's Supreme Soviet adopted a two-year residency requirement for voting rights in the republic, the Intermovement and the United Council of Production Collectives organized a strike committee.[7] There can be some question whether the subsequent actions should be considered lockouts or strikes, since the organizers were mostly plant directors or mid-level managers. Nevertheless, their effort involved somewhere between 20,000 and 40,000 workers nationwide—between three and four percent of the republic's work force—and shut down a number of All-Union, primarily defense-related, plants in Tallinn.[8]

Since the Intermovement has been seen primarily as a Russian movement, an extended look into the nature of the nationality problem in Estonia may be required here. As we shall see, the Intermovement represents the views of about a third of the non-Estonian population in the republic and, moreover, has an agenda quite different from the purely anti-Estonian program that Western journalists have ascribed to it.

Estonian and non-Estonian relations, never particularly warm, have taken a turn for the worse in the past years (Tables 1 and 2). The population and the Party are splitting along nationality lines. Behind the split are profound differences in social and cultural aspirations and in political attitudes, such as assumptions about the freedom of the press, one-party rule, Soviet history and so forth. All this adds up to a rather muddy situation.

Table 1

EVALUATIONS OF ESTONIAN–NON-ESTONIAN RELATIONS
IN RECENT YEARS

	Estonians (%)			non-Estonians (%)		
	1986	1988	DIFF	1986	1988	DIFF
Relations have improved	22	3	-19	42	8	-34
Relations the same	41	28	-13	44	49	+5
Relations worsened	37	69	+32	14	43	+29

Source: *Eesti Kommunist*, 6, 1988, p.15; based on a survey conducted in November, 1986, and April, 1988.

[7] Vello Pettai, "Draft Law for Local Elections in Estonia Criticized," *Radio Free Europe Research*, August 11, 1989.

[8] Radio Tallinn broadcast, March 15, 1989.

Table 2
EVALUATIONS OF ESTONIAN–NON-ESTONIAN RELATIONS
IN THE FUTURE

	Estonians (%)			non-Estonians (%)		
	1986	1988	DIFF	1986	1988	DIFF
Relations will improve	16	11	-5	58	35	-23
Relations will remain the same	46	34	-12	33	44	+11
Relations will worsen	38	54	+16	9	21	+12

SOURCE: *Eesti kommunist*, 6, 1988, p.15; based on a survey conducted in November, 1986, and April, 1988.

A few words on how Estonia fared in the pre-*perestroika* era are in order here. Before World War II, Estonia was 92 percent Estonian. Within the confines of its present borders (Moscow detached a part of the republic in 1944 and incorporated it into the RSFSR), it was 97 percent Estonian. According to studies by Tonu Parming of the University of Maryland, the country lost a quarter of its population during World War II. Immediately following the war, Stalin began a massive program of russification of the country as well as continued depopulation through mass deportations. These are generally viewed by the Estonians as Russian actions against their nation.[9]

Russification dropped off somewhat with the end of Stalinist terror, but only for a while. Under Brezhnev, the country was subjected to new russification, which saw a drastic increase in the numbers of Russians moving into the republic with material privileges—especially in housing—denied to native Estonians. During the Brezhnev era, Moscow also enacted a series of decrees designed to eliminate or circumscribe the use of the Estonian language in everyday life. This campaign became particularly strident in 1978 with the appointment of Party First Secretary Karl Vaino, a Russian of Estonian descent.[10]

An especially significant part of post-war russification policy was the building of large heavy-industry plants in Estonia. The plants required labor and raw materials from outside labor-short Estonia, but shipped the manufactured goods out of the republic. Large housing developments were built to house these non-Estonian workers, and labor to build the housing developments also had to be imported into Estonia, as did person-

---

[9] Tonu Parming, "Population Processes and Nationality Issues in the Soviet Baltic," *Soviet Studies*, XXXII (July, 1980), 398–414; and Tonu Parming, *Population Studies*, XXVI (March, 1972), 53–78.

[10] Toomas Ilves, "Party First Secretary Replaced."

nel required to staff the economic and social infrastructure—the new schools and hospitals needed to serve the builders and workers brought into the country. As a result of this vicious circle, Estonia was inundated by hundreds of thousands of immigrant laborers and their families, and the country developed two completely parallel social structures: an Estonian-language group, with a high percentage of people in white-collar and service jobs, and a Russian-language group, heavily weighted on the unskilled-laborer end. These difficulties are mirrored in Table 3, which shows Estonian and non-Estonian cultural attitudes as reflected in book-reading habits, theater attendance, television viewing and so forth.[11]

To understand the current Intermovement impasse in Estonia, it is especially important to recognize that we are dealing with two very

Table 3

NATIONALITY DIFFERENCES IN ATTITUDES TOWARD CULTURE

	ESTONIANS (%)	NON-ESTONIANS (%)
Own a painting, lithograph or other work of art	54	27
Have library of more than 300 books	38	23
(among workers)	24	9
Attend theater:		
often (> once a month)	33	17
rarely (< once a year)	9	20
Read magazines	95	84
Undertake supplementary education in their area of specialization	73	57
Watch three hours or more of TV a day	29	41
Watch whatever happens to be on TV	7	14
18- to 30-year-olds who read at least four newspapers	20	7
18- to 30-year-olds who read no newspapers	3	15
Those over 40 who read books	90	80
Consider an unpolluted environment important	94	25
Do not consider an unpolluted environment important	1.6	12

SOURCE: ESSR Academy of Sciences Institute of History Survey, published in *Rahva Haal*, October 16, 1987.

---

[11] *Rahva Haal*, October 16, 1987.

different political cultures, with widely differing attitudes on key issues. Only ten percent of Estonians see themselves as members of the Soviet "nation," while fully 78 percent of Russians see themselves so (see Tables 4, 5 and 6). According to a study by Kaarel Haav, seven percent of Russians living in Estonia consider themselves to live in the "Estonian SSR" (as opposed to the USSR), while only two percent of ethnic Estonians, the

Table 4
NATIONAL IDENTITY

	ESTONIANS (%)	RUSSIANS (%)
Identify self as member of national group	73	15
Identify self as member of "Soviet nation"	10	78

SOURCE: *Vikerkaar*, 5, 1988, p. 76.

Table 5
SENSITIVITY TO NATIONALITY

	ESTONIANS (%)	RUSSIANS (%)	OTHERS (%)
Coworkers' nationality is important	80	40	46
Neighbors' nationality is important	82	37	46

SOURCE: *Vikerkaar*, 5, 1988, p. 77.

Table 6
ATTITUDES TOWARD WORK

	ESTONIANS (%)	RUSSIANS (%)	OTHERS (%)
I do only what is required of me	16	30	24
I do somewhat more than required	18	24	28
I try to work as well as possible	66	46	48

SOURCE: *Vikerkaar*, 5, 1988, p. 77.

already linguistically russified portion of the Estonian population, feel at home anywhere in the Soviet Union.

Such differences in nationality identification have immediate consequences in one of the major sore points of nationality relations—the language issue. Indeed, one of the main sources of Intermovement's discontent has been the passage, in January, 1989, of an Estonian SSR language law making Estonian the state language and stipulating the realms in which knowledge of Estonian is a job requirement.[12]

As a result of 45 years of russification, Estonians are quite "internationalized." Ninety-two percent of Estonians know Russian either fluently or adequately enough for everyday needs (Table 7). For Russians and other nationalities, the figures for Estonian knowledge are 38 and 40 percent. Of those migrants who have lived in Estonia for ten or fewer years, ten percent can get by with Estonian, while 45 percent only know Russian. Even more disturbing to Estonians is the fact that of those Russians who have lived in Estonia for over 25 years—or since birth—about 25 percent do not understand Estonian at all. Among Estonians, only two percent know only one language, while 27 percent of Russians know only their own language.[13]

Table 7

SECOND-LANGUAGE KNOWLEDGE IN ESTONIA

	ESTONIANS RUSSIAN LANG. (%)	RUSSIANS ESTONIAN LANG. (%)	OTHERS ESTONIAN LANG. (%)
Completely fluent	25	12	12
Adequate	67	26	28
Understand but do not speak	5	24	17
Know none at all	3	35	37
Unanswered	—	3	—

SOURCE: *Vikerkaar*, 5, 1988, p. 74.

---

[12]   On attitudes toward the language issue and franchise, see Vello Pettai, "Draft Law for Local Elections in Estonia Criticized," *Radio Free Europe Research*, August 11, 1989. Estonian response to political and language questions was shown in the support given to the Citizens' Committees, which would provide immediate franchise only to those who were citizens in 1940 and their descendants. See Vello Pettai, "Estonian Citizens' Committees to Organize Congress of Estonian Citizens," *Radio Free Europe Research*, July 7, 1989.

[13]   *Vikerkaar*, May 5, 1988.

These differences have had direct consequences in such domains as medicine and police work. In Tallinn's Lasnamae Polyclinic, for example, serving one of the largest residential areas in the city, 144 out of 205 nurses know no Estonian and 67 of 126 doctors can speak only Russian to their patients. Sixty percent of pediatricians in Estonia know no Estonian, which obviously has rather Darwinian implications for small Estonian children. Among the militia in Tallinn, a city that is roughly half Estonian, only 17 percent of the police force consists of Estonian-speakers. Virtually all police work is done in Russian, with the result that police often cannot perform their duties.[14]

Faced with such a catastrophic situation, the Estonian SSR adopted the January, 1989, language law that now has become the source of such tension in the republic. Similar conditions in Moldavia have resulted in the passage there of a much weaker law—with, however, no lesser amount of social tension.[15]

But while the Intermovement's opposition to language laws and other Estonian efforts at national reassertiveness can be expected because of nationality considerations, a far more important dimension of fundamental political polarization is illustrated in a poll conducted in April, 1989, in Estonia and summarized in Tables 8–10.[16] Especially striking are the nationality differences in political attitudes. Native Estonians are markedly more liberal regarding political pluralism and frankly anti-communist: in democratic elections in a multiparty system, the Communist Party would come in at fifth place with a dismal seven percent of the vote. The non-Estonian population, on the other hand, is quite conservative, giving the

Table 8
DO YOU FAVOR ABANDONING THE ONE-PARTY SYSTEM?

	Estonians (%)	non-Estonians (%)	Together (%)
Yes, completely in favor	58.0	22.8	45.1
Generally in favor	21.7	20.7	21.3
Generally against	2.6	7.4	4.3
Completely against	1.2	9.5	4.2
Difficult to say	16.0	37.3	23.8
Did not answer	0.5	2.3	1.8

SOURCE: *Ilta Sanomat*, May 3, 1989.

14 *Tallina Ohtvleht*, March 18, 1987.
15 *Rahva Haal*, October 6, 1988.
16 *Ilta Sanomat*, May 3, 1989.

Table 9
WHICH ESTONIAN MOVEMENT, ORGANIZATION OR PARTY WOULD YOU VOTE FOR IN PARLIAMENTARY ELECTIONS?

	ESTONIANS (%)	NON-ESTONIANS (%)	TOGETHER (%)
Communist Party	7.2	32.2	16.3
Popular Front	50.3	8.9	35.2
Greens	12.6	11.5	12.2
Estonian National Independence Party	9.6	0.9	6.4
Rural Union	7.5	4.1	6.3
Estonian Historical Preservation Society	6.0	0.3	3.9
Estonian Christian Union	2.4	0.6	1.7
Union of Work Collectives	0.9	5.9	2.3
Joint Council of Work Collectives	0.2	17.8	7.0
Intermovement	0.0	10.9	4.7
No answer	3.4	6.8	4.7

SOURCE: *Ilta Sanomat*, May 3, 1989.

Table 10
SUMMARIES OF ORGANIZATION RESULTS

	ESTONIANS (%)	NON-ESTONIANS (%)	TOGETHER (%)
Estonian-led groups (except CP)	88.6	32.2	68.0
Pro-independence groups	18.0	1.8	12.0
Russian nationalist groups	0.9	28.7	11.7

SOURCE: Based on *Ilta Sanomat*, May 3, 1989.

largest percentage of its votes (32.2) to the communists. Second place, 17.8 percent, went to the Joint Council of Work Collectives, which is even more conservative than the Estonian Communist Party.

Asked whether they were in favor of a multiparty system, roughly 80 percent of Estonians—but only 43 percent of non-Estonians—said they would support abandoning one-party rule.[17] Sixteen percent of Estonians

---

[17] *Ibid.*

and 37 percent of non-Estonians were not sure. Only four percent of Estonians were against abandoning one-party rule, the same figure, incidentally, as there are Communist Party members among Estonians. Among non-Estonians, 17 percent were against abandoning one-party rule.[18]

As one would expect, Estonians and non-Estonians also differ on such fundamental questions as independence. As Table 11 shows, there is a clear division of attitudes along nationality lines: 54.1 percent of non-Estonians, but a mere 2.4 percent of native Estonians, envision the maintenance of the status quo. These figures are almost exactly reversed on an independent Estonia. Noteworthy also is the support among Estonians and non-Estonians alike for at least a major reorganization of political power within the Soviet Union, with nearly 40 percent of the Estonians—i.e., just about all of those who do not favor outright secession—in support of a confederation system.

The *Ilta Sanomat* poll data, however, as reflected in Tables 8–12, also suggest a much more important dimension to the interfront phenomenon, and one that has been largely ignored in the Soviet as well as the Western press: namely, that while the Intermovement and its sister organizations enjoy support exclusively among the non-Estonian population, the degree of that support is actually far less than is generally assumed. Indeed, only about a third of the non-Estonian population supports the conservative positions of the "inters."

The varied nature of Estonia's non-Estonian population is illustrated by the summary figure in Table 10 for non-Estonian support of Estonian-led organizations (32.2 percent) and in the wide range of attitudes on the restoration of the independence-era Estonian tricolor, a kind of litmus test

Table 11
HOW DO YOU SEE THE FUTURE OF ESTONIA?

	Estonians (%)	non-Estonians (%)	Together (%)
As a constituent republic of the Soviet Union (i.e., as now)	2.4	54.1	21.3
As a sovereign republic in a Soviet confederation	38.7	25.1	33.8
As an independent Estonia	55.5	5.3	37.1
Don't know	2.7	13.9	6.8
Did not answer	0.7	1.5	1.0

Source: *Ilta Sanomat*, May 3, 1989.

---

[18] *Ibid.*

Table 12
DO YOU SUPPORT THE FLYING OF THE BLUE-BLACK-WHITE FLAG ON
THE TOWER OF THE GOVERNMENT BUILDING?

	Estonians (%)	non-Estonians (%)	Together (%)
Yes	88.1	24.0	64.6
Indifferent	3.2	30.2	13.1
No	6.0*	31.1	15.2
Don't know	2.3	11.8	1.3
No answer	0.3	3.0	1.3

Source: *Ilta Sanomat*, May 3, 1989.

* This reflects the attitude of a number of nationalists that the national tricolor cannot represent a state that is not independent.

of how non-Estonians view Estonian national aspirations. Over 50 percent of non-Estonians either support or are indifferent to the Estonian tricolor, while 30 percent are opposed (this presumably represents the same group that supports the Intermovement, the Union of Work Collectives and the Joint Council of Work Collectives). Subsequent studies also report that the non-Estonian population breaks down into thirds, with one third supporting Estonian efforts toward greater independence from Moscow, the second third supporting the conservative internationalist position and the final third essentially indifferent.

The conservative movement should not, however, be discounted, for while its political support base, according to these statistics, amounts to about ten percent of the Estonian SSR population, it has a considerable amount of power. Most tellingly, despite the proletarian nature of the non-Estonian population, roughly 65 percent of the Intermovement's membership, according to the Party daily, consists of white-collar workers and managers of Estonia's large All-Union industries. Two of the main leaders of the Intermovement, Yevgeny Yarovoi and Lev Shepelevitch, are, respectively, directors of the Dvigatel Machine Plant and the Poogelman Electronics Plant. Both are defense-industry plants; Dvigatel is completely closed to Estonian authorities. Such managerial personnel, of course, are the ones with the most to lose with political and economic reform in Estonia: currently the local authorities have no control over the All-Union plants in Estonia. The language law similarly threatens the plant managers with loss of control. Thus, it should come as no surprise that many of the recent strikes in Estonia against the residency requirement for local Soviet elections were in fact not strikes but lockouts. That the defense-related ministries said nothing about strikes in their own factories or about the losses incurred by the actions (which, with the exception of bus-transport disruption, were realized exclusively outside the republic) also gives one pause.

A number of other intriguing facts suggest that the Intermovement is more than it seems to be. Most telling is the Congress of Deputies elections campaign speech of Estonian KGB chief Karl Kortelainen, a known hard-liner. Recorded and published in the Popular Front newspaper *Vaba Maa*, Kortelainen's speech voiced support for all of Intermovement's positions except for its most outrageous, irredentist demand that northeastern Estonia and Tallinn be annexed to the Leningrad oblast of the RSFSR and its insistence that the entire Estonian Communist Party leadership be purged (Kortelainen said only some members should be purged).[19] Otherwise, the KGB chief endorsed the Intermovement platform, condemning the Estonian language law, economic self-management, the Popular Front, etc. Most interestingly for a figure known for his rigorous prosecution of dissidents for "anti-Soviet agitation and propaganda," Kortelainen also urged his listeners not to heed those decisions of local Party committees they didn't like.

Other factors also point to a coordinated conservative effort. The printing of Intermovement material in Leningrad and other places as well as the high degree of cooperation among the various conservative groups could be ascribed to good organization, and the similarity of the August 26, 1989, Communist Party Central Committee declaration on the situation in the Baltic states to Intermovement declarations might simply be due to the political correctness and prescience of the Intermovement.[20] It bears watching, however, that recently a United Council of Production Collectives was founded in Leningrad. This organization, identical to the local Baltic interfronts, obviously has no need to protect Soviet power in Leningrad, the once and future home of Leninist internationalism. Leningrad did, however, reject virtually all of its conservative deputies in the Congress of Deputies elections in the spring of 1989.

If we remove the national element from all of these organizations, they still have a good deal in common: they are opposed to territorial *khozraschet* and the decentralization of economic and political power, and their leaderships consist of conservative middle-level apparatchiks and managers. They have the support of conservative Moscow figures, and their rhetoric corresponds with that of Yegor Ligachev and defense industry leaders as well as the conservative, middle-level apparatchiks who mounted the July 18, 1989, Central Committee attack on Gorbachev. The movements are

---

[19] *Vaba Maa*, March 1, 1989.
[20] TASS, August 27, 1989.

anti-intellectual (the intelligentsia is the main source of reformist thinking in the Soviet Union) and make much of their proletarianism, despite their distinctly management-derived leaderships.

Thus, while the interfronts may appear to be potential breeding grounds for populist anti-Gorbachev sentiment based on Russian nationalism, they may simply be reactions to the decentralizing tendencies that began first in the periphery. But it may be more complex than the mere fact that the devolution of economic—and hence political—power coincides in the case of the Baltic with the rise of nationalism and a reduction in the privileged status of the Russian population. Time may in fact show that interfront-type organizations represent a coming wave of conservative popular organizations, as paradoxical as that may seem. But then again, the Soviet Union is a land of paradoxes.

7

Moscow, Economics and the Baltic Republics

Andris Trapans

Mikhail Gorbachev's program of reform for the economy of the Soviet Union is in its fifth year, having undergone a major and ambitious expansion at the June, 1987, Central Committee plenum, when new and significant parts of the reform package were introduced. Since that time, other reforms have been added, notably the proposed statute for increasing republic rights in planning and management (March, 1989) and the proposed statute for placing all three Baltic states on *khozraschet* (July, 1989).

Altogether, sweeping changes have been introduced that affect most of the economy. These include new and changed planning procedures, a major shake-up of the bureaucracy, significant decentralization of foreign trade, an overhaul of the wage and salary structure, self-financing for a variety of institutions and introduction of private enterprise in agriculture and consumer services. To be sure, some of this has been mostly talk. Little has been done to deration supplies, and the long-heralded price reform is still pending. Parts of the reform package are thus out of alignment with other parts. Still, despite the shortcomings in its execution, the magnitude of the intention cannot be denied. Major conferences are still to be held, and some decisions are yet to be announced. Indeed, if the reform program were to be compared to a stage play, then at present we are somewhere in Act II and not at the end of the play. In other words, it is too early to make a judgment as to how the play will end. But even if prudence dictates caution, the question still ought to be asked: how will Gorbachev's game plan affect the Union republics and particularly the Baltic states? Will it further their endeavors to achieve real economic autonomy? And perhaps more importantly, how do Moscow's offers match the Balts' demands?

In addressing these questions, it is good to keep in mind the sensible viewpoint of Janos Kornai, the well-known Hungarian economist. According to Kornai, there are no "economic-reform supermarkets" in which one can wander around and select only the parts that contain "advantageous qualities."[1] There is a great temptation to do this, not only for outside observers looking in but also for the people on the spot. Demands and expectations in the Baltic states are running far ahead of Soviet reform reality, with the local populations increasingly nationalist. Janos Kornai reminds us that every economic reform is a system that is an organic whole, and that it contains features that may be good or bad.

A simple way of looking at the Gorbachev reform program is to analyze it first in terms of the basic mechanism for resource allocation, and then in terms of the basic principle of partitioning the economy in order to plan and manage it. Once this is done, the implications of the reform package for the Baltic states should become clear.

One way to distinguish among economic systems is by differentiating them according to the prevalent social mechanism for resource allocation. Let us therefore imagine a straight line and call one end of this line a command economy and the other end a socialist market economy, with mixes in between. The command versus socialist market dichotomy is the only one needed for distinguishing among the economies Eastern Europe possessed (and is attempting to escape), because there are no alternative systems (such as a capitalist market or a primitive traditional economy) in this part of the world.

A command economy is one in which resource allocation does not take place through the market and individual enterprises are not guided by the profit motive.[2] Instead, enterprises are told by a central authority what to do—what, when, where, how and how much to produce and consume. These commands are directives and plan targets, and they are derived from a conscious attempt at central state planning. In a command economy, an enterprise therefore has little scope to exercise autonomous choice and is more or less an executor of orders that flow down a vertical bureaucratic hierarchy.

This conceptual sketch is familiar enough: all Stalinist economies are command economies. Although they are still predominantly command economies, some East European economies today are attempting to move away from this heritage; the Soviet Union is also planning and talking

---

[1] Cited by Alec Nove, *The Soviet Economic System*, 3rd. ed. (Boston: Allen Unwin, 1986), 336.

[2] Throughout this chapter, an *enterprise* is understood to refer to any kind of basic business organization—enterprise, production association, *kolkhoz, sovkhoz,* construction organization, industrial association, etc.

about such moves. It is probably Albania that has been least affected by reforms and thus may have the longest surviving pure command economy in Eastern Europe.[3]

A socialist market economy, on the other hand, is one in which productive assets are still mainly owned by the state (hence socialist) but resource allocation takes place through the market. In this kind of economy, enterprises are guided by the profit motive, and they themselves decide, by and large, what, when, where, how and how much to produce and consume. Moreover, they do so largely with reference to the terms on which alternatives are offered, that is, to prices. Naturally, for the mechanism to function properly, the prices themselves have to respond well to the forces of supply and demand and to reflect relative scarcities.[4]

In a socialist market economy, there is little need for central planning and the kind of vast bureaucratic superstructure that makes its living by issuing orders. A socialist market by its very nature means decentralization. The dominant pattern of relationships and communications is a horizontal one, among buyers and sellers in markets for resources and goods. To be sure, the state still retains control over strategic types of investment, but its main task is regulation of economic activity through fiscal and monetary policy.

This system is the obvious alternative to the command economy. Indeed, bits and pieces of the socialist market economy have been present in nearly all East European economic reforms in the past 30 years. However, up until the fall of 1989, there were only two economies that legitimately could be called socialist market economies—Yugoslavia's and Hungary's. Yugoslavia gave birth to the socialist market economy in the 1950s, while Hungary introduced a weaker form of it in 1968. A third socialist market economy, Ota Sik's design for Czechoslovakia, died in the Soviet invasion that followed the "Prague Spring."

The question may now be asked: where is the Gorbachev reform program tending in terms of the command versus socialist market dichotomy, and what does this imply for the Baltic states?

Clearly, it is a movement from a command economy in the direction of a socialist market economy, but one that hesitates and halts before reaching it. It may well be that in the future there will be additional reform measures,

---

[3] For ramifications and details of the command versus socialist market economy dichotomy, see Gregory Grossman, "Notes for a Theory of the Command Economy," *Soviet Studies*, XV (May, 1960), 101–123; and Heinz Kollerz, *Comparative Economic Systems* (Glenview and London: Scott, Foresman and Co., 1989), Chapters 5, 6 and 9.

[4] I.e., they should be a real-world approximation of equilibrium prices and scarcity prices.

more radical than those that have been announced so far; but the current measures would simply create a hybrid system, where patches of socialist market elements (with some simple private areas permitted) are intertwined with a strong lattice of central plans and directives. Indeed, the image conveyed by Soviet reform provisions is one of a two-tier economy, with one tier marketized and the other not.[5]

For example, prices for the more important products would continue to be set centrally and their levels controlled by the state, while another part of prices would be fixed by the enterprises or contractually with their customers. Over time, the share of prices that would be set free to find their own market equilibrium levels would increase, while the share of state-controlled and fixed prices would decrease.

In the area of production planning, the present obligatory targets covering an enterprise's entire range of output would be replaced by a system of "non-binding" control figures and mandatory state orders for one portion of output; another part of output would be produced simply on the basis of customer orders as they come in through sales channels. As with prices, the share of output that is produced according to customer orders would increase over time, while the state-order part would be reduced.

In the supply area, the more scarce goods would continue to be rationed out by the state, while other supplies would be distributed through wholesale trade channels—that is, there would be free purchase (and sale) of a part of inputs. Again, over time, the share of inputs obtainable through market channels would increase, while the centrally allocated share would decline. And so on. The analogy here is of a man standing on two legs, first leaning on one and then on the other. At first the "command" leg would be the more important one; later, as the reform measures take hold, the "market" leg would become the dominant one. This, at least, is the intention of the reformers.

These moves are to be combined with a good deal of administrative decentralization, reducing (but not abolishing) the giving of instructions by

---

[5] The discussion in this section is substantially based on the following sources: "Osnovnye polozheniia korennoi perestroiki upravleniia ekonomiki," *Ekonomicheskaia Gazeta* (July, 1987); John E. Tedstrom, "On Perestroika: Analyzing the 'Basic Provisions,'" *Problems of Communism*, XXXVI (July–August, 1987), 93–98; Joint Economic Committee, Congress of the United States, *Gorbachev's Economic Plans*, I–II (Washington, D.C.: U.S. Government Printing Office, 1988); U.S. Central Intelligence Agency and U.S. Defense Intelligence Agency, *Gorbachev's Economic Program: Problems Emerge* (Washington, D.C.: U.S. Government Printing Office, 1988); and "Visparigie principi savienoto republiku ekonomikas un socialas sferas vadibas parkartosanai uz to suvereno tiesibu paplasinasanas, pasparvaldes un pasfinansesanas pamata," *Cina*, March 15, 1989.

the top authorities, and streamlining and rationalizing (but not dismantling) the State Planning Committee, Gosplan, and the central ministries. Thus, while it is true that some of the Moscow ministries are being dissolved and merged, more than two dozen will still remain.[6] The scope and detail of plans is to be reduced, but the principle of "stable" five-year plans remains.

As many institutions as possible will be placed on *khozraschet*, a term that can be rendered in English as "economic accountability" or "self-financing." An entity functioning according to the principles of *khozraschet* is not subsidized; it is expected to be financially self-supporting and enjoys a measure of financial autonomy. *Khozraschet* institutions are supposed to practice "businesslike management" and are given more normative types of assignments.[7] The role of various financial levers and credit (and hence the banking system) is slated to increase substantially, although the banking changes will be gradual. Soviet reform documents generally project an image of autonomous, self-financing socialist enterprises, freed from the petty tutelage of ministries and involved in markets and competition. This is something quite new in the Soviet Union.[8]

At the same time, it is evident that the central authorities are preserving their right to intervene in local management matters. There is still a ladder of agencies above the enterprise, and these agencies still dispose of an array of central-planning instruments—plans, control figures, "stable" norms, investment "limits," state production orders and so forth. It may therefore be asked: what enterprises, if any, will have the opportunity of making key input and output decisions themselves and working outside the plan?

The answer would seem to be not many, at least in the Baltic states. Gorbachev's reform program does provide for some private and cooperative ownership of productive assets, and a private and quasi-private sector has appeared in the Baltic area—leasehold farms in the countryside and family firms and production cooperatives in the cities. These produce food and provide some consumer services—taxi transportation, hairdressing, appliance repairs and the like. They also offer some small-scale construc-

---

[6] "Par grozijumiem PSRS likuma 'Par PSRS Ministru Padomi,'" *Cina*, July 7, 1989. The text of the decree published names of 26 All-Union economic ministries that are to be retained.

[7] *Normative* controls are less centralized than *directive* ones. An example may serve to illustrate this point. When enterprise wage expenditures are controlled by directive, it tells the enterprise that given its output plan, it is allowed to spend one million rubles in wages. A normative control would be one that says it may spend 20 rubles for every 100 rubles of output. Normative controls increase enterprise autonomy somewhat.

[8] See "Latvijas PSR ekonomiskas patstavibas koncepcija," *Cina*, June 4, 1989.

tion services and manufacture simpler types of consumer goods such as furniture and clothing. This sector can probably make most key production decisions itself, but it is more or less peripheral and reminiscent of similar private and quasi-private sectors that have existed for many years in the satellite states.

There are also some new types of hybrid enterprises such as the larger production cooperatives and joint ventures with foreign firms; these also seem to have a freer hand. However, most enterprises are still state enterprises, and for them the changes do not seem to amount to much. For them, plans and state controls will be looser and the zone of their autonomous initiative broader, but the plans and the vertical structure of the directives will still predominate. In addition, some important marketizing elements of the reform package are lagging behind schedule. Price reforms have been delayed, although prices, more than anything else, have to be the signals that guide enterprise decisions. Derationing of supplies is also lagging, with some Baltic documents implying that the original 1991–92 goals have been pushed back to as late as 1997–98.

Admittedly, some developments are truly new and have potentially significant implications. The republics and local institutions formerly had been cut off (except in cases where Moscow specifically allowed it) from foreign markets and foreign sources of supply. The new reform measures give foreign-trade rights to republics and to specific enterprises. Although much of foreign trade is still under centralized control, the result still will be a development of local linkages with foreign markets and simple technology transfers from abroad.

By early 1989, there were about 30 joint-venture agreements with foreign firms in the Baltic states.[9] This may well be a harbinger of things to come. There have been rumors about the Baltic area becoming a "Soviet Hong Kong," a region for large-scale pilot experiments with foreign-trade reforms. Although there is nothing so far in reform announcements that would substantiate such intentions, Moscow *is* planning some small-scale enterprise and export-processing zones in selected coastal and border areas. The first one is being established near Vyborg on the Finnish-Soviet border, and other ones are under consideration for the Pacific coastal area. These are small strips of land with no customs duties and with special rules to attract foreign investment in factories producing for the export market.[10] If similar zones were to be established somewhere in the Baltic states, it certainly would be novel, but the impact would be modest.

---

[9] Estimate based on roster of "Details of Joint Ventures in the Soviet Union," published in *Business East Europe*, 1988 and 1989 issues.

[10] "Soviets Planning Economic Zones to Draw More Foreign Investment," *Wall Street Journal*, May 2, 1989.

By and large, the marketizing elements in the Gorbachev reforms do not seem to promise major gains for the Baltic states. There should be a somewhat better calibration of supply to the demand of goods and services and some rationalization of resource use. There should be some improvement in the speed and responsiveness of decisions by moving management's center of gravity closer to the actual production process. There also should be increased output of consumer services and small-scale consumer goods through the new private and quasi-private sector, and potentially a major increase in the output of food, if the leasehold-farming system can be implemented on a larger scale. But these are not dramatic changes.[11]

In evaluating the Gorbachev reforms, it will be useful now to turn to another concept. Let us imagine a second straight line showing two basic ways of partitioning the economy in order to plan and manage it. One end point of the line will indicate a purely product-line partitioning and the other a purely territorial one, with mixes in between.

An economy partitioned along product lines is sliced vertically along branch-of-industry lines. In a planning sense, it deals with national-economic product groups. In a management sense, the partitioning also broadly corresponds to product groups, with each one given administrative embodiment through a national ministry. Central control itself might be tight and detailed (in a command economy) or loose and decentralized, focusing only on key priorities (in a socialist market economy).

Historically, it can be said that almost all East European economies have been organized along product lines, since this has suited their planning methods—planning specific products on a national scale in physical terms by the so-called material balances. If in architecture it can be said that form follows function, then in traditional Soviet-type economies it may well be that management form has simply followed planning function.[12]

---

[11] Legal issues aside, two reform measures have to be implemented to make leasehold farming attractive to the population: the prices of farm products have to be increased significantly to make farming profitable, and the farms have to be provided with agricultural machinery suitable to family enterprise. The agricultural machinery presently available is suited only to giant collective and state farms. For a description of the first leasehold farms in Latvia, see "Latvian Family Farm Is Back, Challenging Soviet Collective," *New York Times*, August 18, 1989.

[12] On product-line vs. territorial dichotomy and difficulties with product-line planning in a territorial partitioning of the economy, see Michael Keren, "Industrial vs. Regional Partitioning of Soviet Planning Organizations: A Comparison," *Economics of Planning*, IV (1964), 143–160; Andris Trapans, "Research Possibilities on Soviet Industrial Management" (Santa Monica, Ca.: RAND Corp., 1966); and Andris Trapans, "A Study of Soviet Industrial Administration: The Sovnarkhoz Experiment 1957–65" (University of California, Berkeley: Ph.D. dissertation, 1978).

In the Soviet case, the very pronounced partitioning of the economy along product lines has led to a striking neglect of the territorial dimension in planning and management. In Soviet planning literature, there are abundant examples of a variety of structural and locational problems caused by a near-absence of effective regional planning. Despite many years of talk about "interbranch plans" and "complex programs" for republics and regions, these have remained, for the most part, plans on paper rather than guides to executive action. In the Union republics— including the Baltic states—this has led to great difficulties for the leaderships to deal with their republics as coherent wholes, and even to visualize them as such. Instead, each republic simply appears to be a collection of slices of Moscow-subordinated ministries and planning sectors.[13]

An economy partitioned along territorial lines is divided horizontally into geographical regions, with each region becoming the basic planning and management unit. The boundaries of such regions normally correspond to internal political boundaries—indeed they should correspond to such boundaries, if the arrangement is to be an effective one from the point of view of policy execution.

Central control again could be tighter (in a command economy) or looser and relaxed (in a socialist market economy). Throughout the 1980s, Yugoslavia's was the only example of a socialist market economy partitioned along territorial lines. Its constituent parts were the nationality republics, which had broad autonomy in directing their own development, while Belgrade concerned itself with regulatory policies and broad national priorities and relationships.

When it comes to command economies organized according to the territorial principle, the analogy that comes to mind here is COMECON, somehow transplanted on an internal scale in the Soviet Union. (The Soviet economic reform of 1957 had significant elements of this.) Each of its regions would then be run separately like a mini-economy, conducting "internal foreign trade" with other regions, with the center serving as the interregional balancer and adjudicator. It should be noted, though, that a command economy partitioned according to the territorial principle is not amenable to detailed national product planning, which somehow would have to be reduced and modified.[14]

---

[13] For background and ramifications of these problems, see Trapans, "A Study of Soviet Industrial Administration," Chapters 1 and 2; and Hans Gramatzki, *Räumliche Aspekte der sowjetischen Wirtschaftsplanung* (Berlin: Osteuropa Institut, 1974). On the management problems that a product-line partitioning of the economy generates in Lithuania, see Augustinas Idzelis, "Institutional Response to Environmental Problems in Lithuania," *Journal of Baltic Studies*, XIV (Winter, 1983), 296–306.

[14] See Keren, "Industrial vs. Regional Partitioning."

Small Soviet republics like the Baltic states would seem to be good candidates for implementing the territorial principle. They are large enough to be viable mini-economies but at the same time small enough to be manageable. In contrast, many provinces in the interior of the Soviet Union are too small and undeveloped to be viable economic units, while a republic like the RSFSR is too large and unwieldy to be managed as a single entity.[15]

In terms of the production vs. territorial principle, we may then ask: what do Gorbachev's reforms promise? All of the pieces of the puzzle are not in yet, but what has been recently debated and proposed in Moscow provides some idea. Basically, the intention is to move away from an almost entirely product-line partitioning of the economy to one where the product-line principle is still dominant but where there are also significant and perhaps major territorial elements, with the republics serving as policy loci.

How is this to be accomplished? First of all, there will be a new division of responsibilities. Details of these arrangements still remain to be hammered out, but the general thrust is to place agriculture and food production, the service industries, housing and most consumer-goods production under republic control. At the same time, fuels, basic inputs, heavy and defense industries as well as high-technology industries will still be managed by the central ministries in Moscow, and so will the national transportation nets. In some fields, there will be split jurisdiction—the construction industry will, it appears, be mostly under republic control, but foreign trade for the most part will be under central control. For the Baltic states, this means that the share of enterprises under republic jurisdiction will greatly increase. According to one projection, the output share attributable to enterprises subordinated to the three republics will increase from the present seven to nine percent to 57 to 72 percent, depending on the specific republic. The remaining share (28 to 43 percent) will still be controlled by the central ministries in Moscow.[16]

---

[15] The following discussion is substantially based on these sources: "Pervyi shag k respublikanskomu khozraschetu," *Izvestia*, July 27, 1989; and "Visparigie principi savienoto republiku ekonomikas un socialas sferas vadibas parkartosanai uz to suvereno tiesibu paplasinasanas, pasparvaldes un pasfinansesanas pamata," *Cina*, March 15, 1989. This is the provisional statute for republic management and planning rights. For Latvian statements, see M. Bronsteins, "Musu republikas variants," *Literatura un maksla*, April 15, 1989; Lina Tenison, "Ekonomika un tautvaldiba," *Atmoda*, June 12, 1989; and A. Kalnins, "Savienotas republikas ekonomiska patstaviba," *Cina*, June 14, 1989. For a Baltic view, see Sara Ginaite, "Cost-Accounting in the Baltic Republics and Prospects for their Economic Independence." Paper presented to the Tenth Conference on Baltic Studies in Scandinavia. Stockholm, June 8, 1989.

[16] "Visparigie principi savienoto republiku [provisional statute for republican management and planning rights] . . . ," *Cina*, March 15, 1989.

In a management sense, this is not a simple arrangement, since republic governments will lack unified authority in their territories. Instead, authority will be split, with all of the coordination problems this entails. It seems that only in the field of environmental protection and pollution control will the republics have the right to issue binding directives to all enterprises within their boundaries.[17]

From a planning viewpoint, the new reform program's aim to enhance and increase the role of territorial planning while still retaining the primacy of branch planning sounds rather contradictory, and probably is. The general intention seems to be to give the republics leeway in planning social development and services as well as the agricultural sector, but at the same time to maintain tighter branch planning in industry. The currently available reform rules and proposals do not provide details of how this would work. However, it may be surmised that each republic would be assigned overall output targets (state orders) and the main indicators for its output mix, so that priorities to guide input flows into the national industrial branches would be observed. Similarly, investment plans assigned to the republics might then consist of overall targets for the volume of construction, but with investment again distributed according to the central authorities' specification of the more important industrial branches and projects. These would then be the fixed points around which republic activities could revolve.

What, then, is to be expected from the territorializing aspects of the reforms? The republics should be able to focus more on the regional aspects of policy formation, which formerly were neglected at considerable cost to the economy. Regional planning is especially suited to resources tied to location—labor, transportation, water, power and the like. There certainly have been all kinds of locational absurdities and resource misuse engendered by the traditional ministerial system. One glaring example is the practice of locating large, high-cost industrial plants in the Baltic states, where they were far removed from both sources of raw materials and markets for their output and frequently also lacked locally available labor.[18] There are also other and less obvious examples of this kind, results of the failure to arrange for the use of joint products or byproducts manufactured by enterprises in the same geographical area but belonging to different ministries.

---

[17] *Ibid.*

[18] This is so well known and so often stressed in Baltic scholarly literature abroad that sources scarcely need to be cited. However, Soviet regional planners have also known for a long time that these absurdities exist. See *Pribaltiskii economis-cheskii raion* (Moscow: Nauka, 1970), particularly the chapter on chemicals, machine-building and production location.

The republics are expected to do something about problems of this kind and to act as general "area rationalizers." But it is not at all clear how far they will be able to proceed, given the awkward management split described earlier. The Balts probably will be best off trying to shape the development of those sectors that now will be primarily managed by the republics—agriculture, services, light industry supplying the local market, a part of foreign trade. Of all these, agriculture and food production are presently regarded as the most important.

There also has been some talk of attempting a general industrial reorientation of the Baltic economies, switching their ties from Russia to the West, but this should be taken with a grain of salt. Not only will a part of the industries in the Baltic states remain under the central ministries' jurisdiction, but there are also long-established supply and delivery linkages to enterprises in the Soviet Union. These cannot simply be cut and the deliveries ended or switched around.

One interesting feature of the reform program is republic *khozraschet*, effective in the Baltic states as of January 1, 1990. Narrowly, this means that from this year on, each republic will have to be financially self-sustaining. In line with this assumption, the Baltic republics will dispose of a part of their tax revenues (perhaps as much as one half) and have some independent fiscal authority. Republic *khozraschet* will also create a modest independent zone of authority and the resources to maneuver in it, endowing the three states with quasi-corporate characteristics.[19] Not just for financial planning and record keeping but for all planning, each republic will be defined as a single, coherent entity and visualized as such by decision makers.

When all is said and done, though, a final fact remains. Although the central ministerial establishment in Moscow is being cut down in size and scope, it will still remain in existence. So will the product-line divisions of Gosplan and its ancillaries. Decisions at the top will still mostly be made in terms of national branches rather than territories.

In the preceding pages, the changes proposed under the Gorbachev reform program were considered in terms of two broad but separate dimensions. It should now be recognized that this is an artificial distinction; they really are not separate. Let us therefore combine the command/ socialist market and the product line/territorial scales into a single reference grid. Once this is done, it becomes evident that four different mixed systems are possible:

---

[19] According to one Baltic economist, the republic *khozraschet* concept was created because there was no Soviet regional economic theory and the concept of an enterprise was simply elevated to the republic level. See the comments by S. Dimans, "Republikas saimnieciskais aprekins: Attistibas alternativas," *Padomju Latvijas Komunists* (December, 1988), 14–18.

TYPE I —Product-line command economy
TYPE II—Product-line socialist market economy
TYPE III—Territorial socialist market economy
TYPE IV—Territorial command economy

What Moscow has offered and what the Balts want can now be analyzed with reference to these system types. TYPE I, the product-line command economy, is familiar enough. It is the traditional Soviet economy from Stalin to Chernenko, and it is the one from which the Gorbachev reforms are trying to move away. The movement, as we have seen, is in the direction of TYPE II, a looser product-line socialist market economy. However, what has taken place and what has been announced so far in Moscow does not yet presage a socialist market economy. The Soviet Union today still has a command economy, albeit one in a preliminary stage of transition, with looser central controls and more local management autonomy. In the next few years (assuming that the reforms announced so far are carried out), it probably would be no more than a halfway-house TYPE I/II. This hybrid would still broadly be run from Moscow, and still for the most part along branch lines, but it would also incorporate significant territorial elements. From the point of view of the Balts, of course, this does not amount to much.

It may now be asked: what do the Baltic Popular Fronts want? These broad nationalist-autonomist groups have become a powerful force for influencing their republic governments, and in all three Baltic states the evolution of their thinking has been similar. Although each of the Popular Fronts has drawn up its own proposals for future reforms, the three have taken care to coordinate their ideas and to present a united front to the authorities in Moscow. We may thus speak of a general Baltic reform consensus, where there are differences in emphasis and details but broad agreement on fundamentals. By late 1988 to early 1989, the Baltic consensus had evolved into an all-out TYPE III—a territorial socialist market economy.[20] In itself, of course, the territorial element of these demands is not surprising—anything that increases and magnifies the territorial principle implies more management for the national territories. What is surprising is the dramatic extent of these demands.

The image conveyed by them is of a Soviet Union that is a confederation in all but name. Each of the Baltic states would have its own money, each would be the sovereign owner of natural resources and productive assets in its land and each would be in charge of virtually all enterprises, managing its territory as a unified complex. There would be a broad mix of state,

---

[20] For the original texts of Baltic proposals, see *Padomju Jaunatne*, September 7 and 15, 1988; *Sovetskaia Estoniia*, September 30 and October 1, 1988; and *Sovetskaia Litva*, October 9, 1988. The proposals were developed by Popular Front economists.

cooperative and private property. Interrepublic exchanges would be anchored in trade agreements, with each republic being more or less its own planner. The center in Moscow would then be reduced to helping balance interrepublic exchanges and supervise joint endeavors requiring mutual coordination in an overall Union market. If something like this were indeed to occur, the Baltic states would still be related to the Soviet economy, but more along the lines of, say, Mongolia.

TYPE III, the all-out territorial socialist market economy, was not to be. Gorbachev angrily called the more extreme proposals "the path of disconnection" that was clearly to be rejected, since the USSR's "future lies not in weakening the ties among the republics but in strengthening and expanding their cooperation."[21] He was not the only one to sound this warning.

In the spring and summer of 1989, what might be called a "Moscow consensus," showing what the Balts could realistically get, appeared. The terminology used was modest—"broadening of republic rights," "self-management," "republic *khozraschet*" and the like, implying no more than a kind of semi-autonomy. A number of proposals seem to have been used in forming the Moscow consensus, some of them published and others apparently not. These included proposals prepared by Gosplan, the Soviet Union Council of Ministers and by the Balts.[22]

Essentially, the central authorities seem to have passed their own version of republic rules, but with some concessions to the Balts. These include accepting the idea of republic *khozraschet*, which was apparently originally developed in Tallinn, and making Estonia, Latvia and Lithuania the first republics to be placed on *khozraschet*. There may also have been concessions to some Baltic requests about property and financial rights, but this is not clear.

What is one to make of Gorbachev's economic reform program insofar as it applies to the Baltic states? It might be wise to avoid drawing any conclusions, for the future is likely to produce additional reforms, grafted on the ones already there. The past is no longer a reliable predictor of Soviet behavior, and outside observers have to learn to expect the unexpected.

---

[21] Gorbachev's response to the Estonian statement on republican sovereignty appeared in *Izvestia*, November 28, 1988. A similar warning was later voiced by USSR Council of Ministers Chairman Nikolai Ryzhkov.

[22] The main document, a provisional statute for republic management and planning rights, was prepared by a committee headed by Gosplan (footnote 15), while proposals by the Balts were significant for republican *khozraschet* (footnote 20). However, there also were other orienting documents, one prepared by the USSR Council of Ministers on general republic reform issues, and the second one dealing specifically with the Baltic states and Belorussia. These apparently were not published. See the comments by Latvian economist A. Kalnins in *Cina*, June 14, 1989.

Still, the reform package visible thus far does lead to some tentative conclusions. For Estonia, Latvia and Lithuania, the most significant and interesting feature is republic *khozraschet*. Although it is present in a more anemic form than the Balts would have wanted, it is something new; it defines each national territory as a single and coherent entity and gives its administrators a frame of reference for making decisions. It is also a financial management tool and compels the republics to be self-sustaining. Although the Baltic states are still Union republics, they are starting to operate according to somewhat different rules from the others. Other republics and regions will be encouraged to copy their *khozraschet*, if and when they are able. However, only the Balts have the *élan vital* provided by their Popular Fronts, in which large groups of economists and lawyers have functioned as informal "think tanks" to develop reform proposals from below. At present no other republics have the ability to harness this kind of intellectual capacity.

Yet much less than the Balts have wanted is being offered them in Moscow. The reform program does introduce elements of a socialist market economy, but at the same time it leaves in place the familiar support posts of central planning, only somewhat changed in form and reduced in size. The program also strengthens the territorial principle at the republic level, but it splits management responsibility, attempting to maintain the primacy of branch planning in Moscow. In this sense, the whole package is neither fish nor fowl. The Balts cannot obtain economic sovereignty through these reforms, which promise no more than a kind of semi-autonomy. This will not satisfy them, to put it mildly.

PART FOUR

The Empire

8

End of Empire, End of Illusions?

Paul B. Henze

It is clear today that Marxism-Leninism as practiced for more than 70 years in the Soviet Union has not only failed to solve ethnic tensions and eliminate nationality concerns as a complicating factor in governing, it has exacerbated them. For a long time this was a debatable issue in the West. The debate was seldom heated, however, because those who considered these questions of little importance, in both academia and government, held the center stage. They were smugly confident of the correctness of their position. No matter that everything that can be learned from the prodigious body of literature on nationalism that has been produced during the past 150 years justifies extreme skepticism about any down-grading of national feeling and its practical ramifications—anywhere, anytime. The Soviet Union was supposed to be different. As long as Brezhnev was alive, the Soviet Union could encourage its operatives and agents to meddle in situations of ethnic conflict in other parts of the world—invariably with the purpose of exacerbating strains and undermin-ing established governments—and feel comfortably insulated from such problems at home. Marxism-Leninism made the difference.

Until three or four years ago, a poll among American scholars specializ-ing in Soviet affairs would probably have produced a majority in favor of the proposition that relations between nationalities in the Soviet Union were only an incidental source of tension in the society and of little importance as a factor in political and economic decision making by the leadership. A majority would probably also have argued that over time such problems as existed would probably decline in significance. Writers and researchers who persisted in examining ethnic and religious issues in depth were tolerated but often regarded as somewhat outside the main-stream of scholarly respectability.

In the Carter Administration, thanks to the persistence of Zbigniew Brzezinski, the US government actually established an interagency subcommittee at the National Security Council level, the Nationalities Working Group, to initiate and monitor research and review operations such as radio broadcasting and cultural exchanges relating to Soviet nationality affairs. The group was disbanded when the Reagan Administration took office, but some of the initiatives it had encouraged during its three brief years in operation fortunately continued and even gained momentum.

Journalists for the most part have a better record on the nationality question than academics. Many of them who lived in Moscow for two or three years and took advantage of the opportunity to travel saw a great deal of evidence of submerged ethnic pride as well as tension (actual or potential), often opposite sides of the same coin. But many discovered their home desks were not particularly interested in a subject regarded as esoteric. They were discouraged from probing deeply or reporting in great detail. How quickly times have changed! It is not uncommon now for the *New York Times* to carry three substantial dispatches on Soviet nationality problems on a single day.

Most specialists in Soviet nationality affairs, on the other hand, would probably confess that even with the benefit of detailed knowledge, historical understanding and appreciation of the emotional dimensions of ethnic issues, they are surprised at the speed with which ferment has developed and situations have become exacerbated. No one dared to predict just a few years ago that demands for secession would be aired publicly and continuously in several republics simultaneously. No one could foresee that organizations championing nationality rights in the Baltic republics would quickly gain far larger memberships than those republics' Communist parties or that republican Communist leaders would find themselves compelled to join the dissident movements to retain their own positions.

All this is for the most part a result of Gorbachev's daring approach to *perestroika*—his tendency to let difficult issues be aired and examined in the hope that people's own perceptions of their concerns will become more rational and that action to correct the dysfunctions in "socialism" thus can be facilitated. Gorbachev appears to have miscalculated. He miscalculated because he is a rationalist and thinks primarily in Marxist-Leninist categories. He still believes that "scientific socialism" is a valid method of analysis and governance—if only people will respect it and leaders practice it conscientiously. In this attitude he is doubly mistaken, for the premises on which "scientific socialism" rests are fundamentally questionable. And even if they were valid, people could not be persuaded to follow them on the basis of rationality alone. National feelings and ethnic attitudes are deeply emotional. Gorbachev's whole life history and professional background provided him with almost no exposure to non-Russian ethnic groups and very little experience of nationalities issues.

The problem goes much deeper than Gorbachev. The difficulty lies with Marxism-Leninism itself. Karl Marx displayed some understanding of religious and ethnic issues when he was writing about the Crimean War and peoples of the Balkans and the Caucasus in the 1850s, but he never penetrated further into what we now call the Third World than Algiers. His fascination with class as the key to understanding societies and devising just governmental systems led him to ignore history, culture, religion and nationalism. Marxism in power has actually exacerbated nationality problems. This exacerbation is fundamental to the system for several interconnected reasons:

First, a Marxist-Leninist system is authoritarian and rigid. Orders and directives flow downward, whereas information actually flows most easily or dependably upward in a form in which it must be taken into account by leaders. Thus, until recently, the Soviet leadership may well have kept itself as ill informed about the seriousness of ethnic tensions (as well as many other critical problems in its society) as Western academics. No longer. Gorbachev's conservative critics berate him for having opened Pandora's box, but sooner or later it would have blown open anyway. Gorbachev is now experimenting with correctives, but the dry rot was deep-seated and cannot be quickly repaired. The best method that has been discovered for ensuring that the flow of information will have political impact is free elections with competing parties. Issues in open societies can be debated and acted upon before they reach acute form.

Second, a Marxist-Leninist system does not produce habits of compromise and accommodation in a population. This is as true of Yugoslavia as it is of the Soviet Union. It produces habits of submission and obedience. Quiescence in such a society is impressive while it lasts—but illusory. People do not forget grievances. When controls are loosened, they burst forth with great strength and in highly emotional form. People fall into irreconcilable confrontations and keep hardening their positions.

Third, the fundamental dishonesty that permeates Marxist-Leninist societies and governments downgrades and undermines the very concept of rational calculation that the leaders pretend underlies all their actions. People suppress their real feelings but not only do not abandon them, they hold onto them more intensely. They develop a proclivity to believe the opposite of anything the leadership tries to force upon them. The notion of *Druzhba Narodov* (peoples' friendship) is not inherently undesirable as a basis for life in a mature multiethnic society, but it has been propagated with so much ostentatious fakery that it appears to the average Soviet citizen as a parody of the reality he experiences every day.

Fourth, it is now evident—for a long time it was not—that Marxism-Leninism in power leads to economic stagnation and a wide range of attendant ills, including rampant corruption. Where everyone is living under conditions of economic stringency, ethnic grievances become intensified and competition for scarce goods and opportunities intensifies. All economic actions take on ethnic overtones. People fall back on family, clan and ethnic connections to gain some marginal advantage or to protect themselves from greater adversity. Grievances feed upon themselves.

Fifth, Stalin's totalitarian system was based on the assumption that Soviet society could be cut off from communication with the outer world, while separate elements within the country could be isolated from each other. By the end of the 1960s, the effort was failing, but Brezhnev had nothing to put in its place. The electronic revolution has advanced with steadily accelerating speed during the 1970s and 1980s. Like so many other features of Soviet policy, the outcome has been a dialectic process: because there was such a long effort to suppress communication with the outer world as well as among Soviet peoples, those peoples have developed greater skill and effectiveness in this process than most free peoples with far greater information resources available to them.

Finally, though all peoples in the Soviet Union were supposed to be treated equally, the non-Slavs were subjected to many kinds of capricious manipulation. Foremost among the victims of the policy of ethnic fragmentation was the largest non-Slavic group in the Soviet Union—the Turks. Not only in Central Asia, where they were gerrymandered into territorial units designed to foster as much localism and particularism as possible, but in the Urals and the North Caucasus, too, the aim was to deprive Turks of any basis for maintaining feelings of ethnic and religious solidarity. This policy has failed. So has the effort to create a separate Moldavian nationality. In the Caucasus, on the other hand, where the Transcaucasian Federation was dissolved in 1936 to keep the three major Transcaucasian peoples from collaborating to serve their own regional interests, the policy of divide and rule has failed in the totally opposite direction—thousands of Georgians, Azerbaijanis and Armenians are, quite literally, at each other's throats. Moscow can no longer cope with the problems their mutual hostilities generate.

Kemal Ataturk is sometimes compared with Lenin. Both were strong-willed, articulate and impressive in their capacity for intellectual leadership, and both were admirers of modern European culture. Statues of Ataturk and streets and squares named after him are as prevalent in Turkey today as monuments of many kinds to Lenin in the Soviet Union. The two men were nevertheless very different, and the legacies they left their countries stand in strong contrast. Ataturk had no desire to reconstitute the

Ottoman Empire. He was content to establish a coherent, non-expansionist nation-state. He was dictatorial in his methods but deeply committed to basic principles of Western civilization, and he aspired to set his people on the path to democracy and a pluralistic society. His legacy is an entirely positive feature of modern Turkish life.

In the name of internationalism, Lenin reestablished the Russian Empire and invented an elaborate mythology claiming that the Soviet Union was a new and higher kind of political entity than the world had heretofore seen. To preserve the "revolution," he instituted all the most odious features of the authoritarian system that Stalin consolidated. Beginning with Khrushchev in 1956, successive Soviet leaders have heaped the blame for everything that has gone awry on Stalin. Those leaders, including Gorbachev, have clung to Lenin, because without him they have no claim to legitimacy. But Lenin's legacy is dubious and increasingly controversial. Could there have been a Stalin without a Lenin?

Of Stalin's negative impact on Soviet history there can be no doubt—and the damage has not yet played itself out. Three of Stalin's actions had important effects on the nationality issue, and the Soviet Union is still struggling with their consequences:

(1) The brutality that accompanied collectivization affected all Soviet peoples adversely, including the Russians, but was particularly severe on two important nationalities: the Ukrainians and the Kazakhs, both of whom occupy large territories essential to the existence of the Soviet Union.

(2) The deportation of several nationalities during World War II cannot be erased from the collective consciousness of Soviet society. Though some of the "punished peoples" were permitted to return to their original territories in the 1950s and 1960s, their resentments continue to run deep. Others who have been kept in exile—the Crimean Tatars, the Volga Germans and the Meskhetians—have become irretrievably alienated from the Soviet system and will continue agitating and/or emigrating, thus setting an example for other disgruntled ethnic groups.

(3) Last but not least, Stalin incorporated the Baltic republics and forced communism on Eastern Europe during and after World War II. The Soviet system was incapable of absorbing these acquisitions; all have proved indigestible, and all have long had an increasing impact on the Soviet Union itself. In the current decade, this process has accelerated steadily. The Balts are now pressing to regain their independence, and Gorbachev's reaction has exposed the voluntary secession provision of the Soviet constitution as fraudulent. The impact of these developments on the Soviet system remains to be seen. For brief periods, this impact may be contained and even arrested, but it cannot be blocked.

All serious students of Soviet nationality problems have long recognized that the central issue is not necessarily one of russification or of Russians against non-Russians and non-Slavic nationalities. Russians and other Slavs have been favored at times in Soviet history, but never for long. Ukrainians have suffered as much from communism as any people in the entire Soviet empire. Belorussians, once thought to have been largely absorbed into Russian culture, have recently displayed remarkable ethnic vitality and assertiveness.

A strong case can be made that the people on whom Marxism-Leninism has inflicted the broadest damage is the Russians themselves. The damage takes many forms: the degeneration of rural life and with it the wellsprings of traditional Russian culture; the moral damage stemming in part from the suppression and manipulation of the Russian Orthodox Church; the demographic damage—Russians have come close to achieving zero population growth; the meager economic gains from decades of exertion and sacrifice; the opprobrium Russians suffer and will continue to suffer from other peoples of the Soviet Union and Eastern Europe for being the sponsors and standard-bearers, willingly or otherwise, of Communist rule.

Glasnost has revealed as much basic dissatisfaction and disillusionment with Marxism-Leninism among Russians as among any other ethnic groups in the Soviet empire. The rise of strong nationalist groups among Russians threatens the system in more fundamental ways than does nationalism among the non-Slavic nationalities. As attractive as in-migrating Russians have found life in the Baltic republics, a process of out-migration is likely to begin and may well be under way. The same is likely in Moldavia and the Ukraine. It has long been observed in Central Asia and the Caucasus and will in all likelihood be found to have accelerated when results of the recent census are thoroughly assessed.

By the time the Ottoman Empire collapsed, there were practically no Turks left to advocate its resuscitation. The very idea would seem ludicrous to Turks today. The Austro-Hungarian Empire slipped into history unmourned. Today it provides grist for writers of historical romances, little more. Many Britons and Frenchmen were upset at the peaceful dissolution of their colonial empires during the 1950s and 1960s, but they were never close to a majority. Democratic societies in the modern world are unlikely to want to bear the costs of empire, even if they are relatively light. Britain and France have preserved cultural, economic and even political links with most of their former colonies, dominions and protectorates by purely voluntary means. Is it too late for any comparable evolution to occur in the Soviet empire, among Russians? This is the most important—now unanswerable—question Russians must face in the years immediately ahead.

Will Russians simply tire of the strain and costs of being an imperial power and let non-Russians go their own way? Will Russians retain their own cohesion across that vast expanse from Petersburg (as more and more insist on calling it) to Vladivostok? There is an enormous amount in their history of which Russians can be proud. They are one of the world's great nations. But they are carrying an unconscionable burden, and there is little promise that they can ever be compensated for the cost of carrying it. It is too early to do more than speculate, but the locomotive of history has been accelerating steadily and could reach the point where decisions, if not taken consciously, will force themselves upon the Russian people.

Gorbachev is confronted with an exquisite dilemma in the Baltic states. He appears to have encouraged their political evolution in hopes that it could be contained and serve as an example for the Soviet Union as a whole. If so, he misestimated badly. But he cannot easily reverse or even restrain the processes he has set in motion. If Stalin had been content to leave the Baltic republics nominally free, like the other countries of Eastern Europe, the problems of dealing with them now would be much easier. They are an example that other constituent republics aspire to follow. Communication among them is good. It could be interfered with but would be very difficult to halt, given the access everyone in the Soviet Union now has to information from abroad. The KGB and the armed forces could be sent in to take power and install puppet leaders in Tallinn, Riga and Vilnius. The task would be much more difficult than it was in Czechoslovakia in 1968. Bloody clashes and mass resistance would be inevitable. The economic losses would be great, for Moscow gains more economically from the Baltic states than they gain from association with the Soviet Union.

The most serious consequences, however, would be in Gorbachev's relations with Europe and the rest of the world. No part of the Soviet empire is felt by Europeans to be as European as the Baltic republics. Their links to Scandinavia and Germany are long-standing and close. The economic support that Gorbachev so desperately needs from Europe would be drastically reduced by any move to suppress dissent in the Baltic states. Gorbachev is thus likely to be happiest if he can persuade the Balts to tone down their rhetoric and go their own way more quietly. The onrush of events and hardening of attitudes may already, however, have made that temporary expedient impossible.

Gorbachev might, of course, fall as a result of controversy in the central power structure over events in the Baltic states and their repercussions in Moldavia and Azerbaijan. The problem would be no easier to solve for a successor. Gorbachev has built his power base by alternating daring personnel shifts and policy moves, exploiting the lack of cohesion among conservative opponents and keeping key elements in the power structure—the KGB and a decisive portion of the military leadership—on his side. This feat could not easily be repeated by a successor. Gorbachev has also created a new institution—the Congress of People's Deputies—that he can use to divide and neutralize opposition from the nomenklatura and the CPSU apparat. His capacity to take positive action has been steadily reduced, but his ability to block action against him is still formidable and should not be discounted. Eliminating Gorbachev might set in motion a process that would lead to the elimination of the Marxist-Leninist system itself.

9

Baltic Echoes in Ukraine

Bohdan Nahaylo

In June, 1923, shortly after the formation of the Soviet Union, there was a candid discussion among officials about the nature of the Soviet multinational state. At the Fourth Conference of the Central Committee of the Russian Communist Party (Bolsheviks) with Responsible Workers of the National Republics and Regions, Stalin complained that "the Ukrainian comrades" were seeking to "obtain in the definition of the character of the Union something midway between a confederation and a federation, with a leaning towards confederation."[1] Six and a half decades later, the wheel of history has turned full circle, only now it is the Estonian, Latvian and Lithuanian "comrades" who have taken the lead in asserting the sovereignty of the national republics and, as Stalin put it in 1923, "trying to force confederation" on Moscow.[2]

The Baltic revolution has had an impact throughout the USSR. One key area where it has influenced developments is Ukraine, the most important non-Russian republic because of its large population and economic clout.

The fundamental issues raised by Baltic activists after *glasnost* had begun to take effect were ones that had concerned Ukrainian dissidents since at least the beginning of the 1960s—the decade in which Ukrainians pioneered legalistic forms of national dissent. It was in 1961 that the jurists Levko Lukyanenko and Ivan Kandyba[3] were given long prison terms for seeking to launch a legal campaign to test Ukraine's constitutional right to

---

[1] J. V. Stalin, *Works* (Moscow: Foreign Languages Publishing House, 1953), Vol. V, 343.

[2] *Ibid.*, 347.

[3] On the so-called "Jurists' group," see Konstantyn Sawchuk, "Opposition in the Ukraine: Seven Versus the Regime," *Survey*, XX (Winter, 1974), 36–46.

secede from the Soviet Union. Four years later, the literary critic Ivan Dzyuba wrote his classic critique of Soviet nationalities policy, *Internationalism or Russification?*, in which he called for the restoration of the sovereignty of the non-Russian republics.[4] A decade later, the unofficial Ukrainian Helsinki monitoring group continued to demand that the proclaimed sovereignty of the Union republics be respected.[5]

The revival of Ukrainian cultural and public life in the 1960s was followed by a bleak period. In 1972–73, a major political and cultural purge inflicted a devastating blow to national life and inaugurated a period of intensified repression and russification.[6] Fifteen years later, when Gorbachev began his new course, the First Secretary of the Communist Party of Ukraine (CPU) was still Brezhnev's former lieutenant Volodymyr Shcherbitsky, who was installed in Kiev in 1972 to rid Ukraine of nationalism, real or imagined.

As in the Baltic republics, it was, apart from the dissidents, Ukraine's writers who first began to probe the limits of the new, more liberal, line and to come out with national grievances and demands. They were among the first to make use of *glasnost* to oppose russification and to press for recognition of the principle that the language of the indigenous population of a Union republic should be made the state language of that republic. After the disaster at the Chernobyl nuclear power station in April, 1986, Ukrainian writers also began speaking out on environmental issues. In Ukraine, again as in the Baltic republics, ecological movements gradually began to take shape.[7]

There were also important differences between the situation in Ukraine and in the Baltic republics. For one, the hold of the conservative Shcherbitsky regime in Ukraine was still strong, as was the sense of fear, powerlessness and national inferiority before all things Russian that the regime had instilled in the population. Moreover, russification and the erasure of national memory had made considerable headway and sharpened the regional differences between Western Ukraine, which had only come under Soviet rule in 1939 and where the level of national consciousness was

---

[4] Ivan Dzyuba, *Internationalism or Russification? A Study of the Soviet Nationalities Problem* (London: Weidenfeld & Nicolson, 1968).

[5] See Bohdan Nahaylo, "Ukrainian Dissent and Opposition After Shelest," in Bohdan Krawchenko, ed., *Ukraine After Shelest* (Edmonton: Canadian Institute of Ukrainian Studies, University of Alberta, 1983), 30–54.

[6] For details, see Bohdan Nahaylo and Victor Swoboda, *Soviet Disunion: A History of the Nationalities Problem in the USSR* (London and New York: Hamish Hamilton, 1990), 177–79, 188 and 207–208.

[7] See Nahaylo and Swoboda, *Soviet Disunion*, 244–45, 251, 261–62, 264–65 and 271–72.

high, and the central and eastern parts of the republic. Not only was there no nationally minded faction within the CPU prepared to support the idea of national regeneration or genuine democratization, but also millions of Ukrainians had been effectively denationalized and reduced to "Little Russians." Consequently, Ukrainian activists could not mobilize the kind of mass support their Baltic counterparts could, and their attention was largely focused on very basic problems connected with raising national consciousness and promoting national integration.

In the second half of 1987, while Ukrainian writers were still concerning themselves with cultural and environmental questions, the Balts added political and economic aspects to their campaign for greater national rights. In Estonia and Latvia, there was already considerable opposition to the inflow of Russian-speaking workers. The turning point came on August 23, 1987, when the 48th anniversary of the signing of the Molotov-Ribbentrop Pact was marked by demonstrations in all three Baltic republics. After this, Baltic activists and, increasingly, representatives of the Baltic creative intelligentsia began to demand that the true history of what had befallen their nations be told and that their national rights be restored. The head of the Latvian Writers' Union, Janis Peters, for instance, stressed in *Pravda* on September 16 that "each Union republic is a sovereign state, with its own constitution, parliament and government, anthem, flag and coat of arms." Later that month, a group of Estonian Communists came out with a radical proposal to turn their republic into a "self-managing economic zone."

When, in the spring of 1988, things really started moving in the Baltic republics, there was a prompt response in Ukraine. At first the Estonians led the way. In early April, the Council of Estonian Cultural Unions adopted two radical resolutions addressed to the forthcoming 19th Conference of the Communist Party and to the Party and government leaders of Estonia. The council demanded the decentralization of the Soviet Union and broad political, cultural and economic autonomy for the republics. Shortly thereafter, on May 8, the Ukrainian weekly *Kultura i zhyttya* suggested on its front page that a similar independent cultural council be established in the Ukraine.[8] The proposal seems to have been quashed behind the scenes, however, for there was no follow-up to this implicit call for emulating the Estonians.

The Ukrainians made other attempts to follow the Balts' lead. On April 13, 1987, Estonian patriots and reformists announced the formation of an Estonian Popular Front in Support of Restructuring. It soon grew into a mass grass-roots movement for genuine democratization, the restoration of national sovereignty and radical decentralization of the Soviet Union.

---

[8] "Bilshe demokratii i hlasnosti," *Kultura i zhyttya*, May 8, 1988.

The Lithuanians set up their own popular movement (Sajudis) on June 3, and later that month the Latvians also began to organize an analogous Latvian Popular Front.

The example set by the Balts was soon being followed in Ukraine. On June 9, 1987, a Popular Union to Promote Restructuring was established in Kiev.[9] That same month there were mass meetings in the Western Ukrainian city of Lvov, one of which, on June 21, drew 50,000 people. The following month, on July 7, informal groups in Lvov launched a Democratic Front to Promote Restructuring at a rally attended by some 20,000 people.[10]

Over the years, considerable solidarity had developed among non-Russian political prisoners in the Soviet Union. It was therefore not surprising that, on being freed as part of the "democratization" process, activists from the various republics sought to maintain and strengthen their links. First— in September, 1987—Ukrainians and Armenians founded a joint committee in defense of political prisoners. By the following summer, this initiative had developed into a more ambitious effort to form a common front of the various non-Russian national movements against Moscow's rule.

On June 11 and 12, 1988, leading national-rights campaigners from the Ukraine, Armenia, Georgia, Lithuania, Latvia and Estonia met in Lvov and established a Coordinating Committee of the Patriotic Movements of the Peoples of the Soviet Union. Although those who took part in the meeting were primarily advocates of political independence for their respective nations, they adopted a programmatic position suited to the conditions of restructuring and "democratization." Their position resembled the goal proclaimed by the Popular Fronts that had recently emerged in the Baltic republics, namely "the complete political and economic decentralization of the Soviet Union" and the transformation of the Soviet Union into "a confederation of separate sovereign states."[11]

By the time the 19th All-Union Party Conference opened in Moscow on June 28, the dynamic Baltic national movements had succeeded in forcing the Party leaders in all three Baltic republics to take some of their demands into account. In fact, on the eve of the conference, public pressure had toppled Estonia's "Shcherbitsky," Karl Vaino. Consequently, at the conference itself, the Baltic representatives pressed for the expansion of the rights of the Union republics and for the transformation of the Soviet Union into a genuine federation.

---

[9] *Russkaya mysl*, June 24 and July 15, 1988.

[10] See Roman Solchanyk, "Democratic Front to Promote *Perestroika* Formed in the Ukraine," *Radio Liberty Research Bulletin*, No. 324, July 17, 1988.

[11] See Bohdan Nahaylo, "Representatives of Non-Russian National Movements Establish Coordinating Committee," *Radio Liberty Research Bulletin*, No. 283, June 22, 1988.

Sympathy and support for what the Estonians, Latvians and Lithuanians were doing were not restricted to Ukrainian dissidents and unofficial groups. It was clear from some of the speeches made in July at the joint plenum of the board of the Ukrainian Writers' Union and the board of its Kiev section how impressed the Ukrainian literary community was with the stance taken by the Baltic delegates at the 19th Party Conference.[12] The Ukrainian literary community was still leading the campaign for change in Ukraine.

After the 19th Party Conference, the mass patriotic movements in the Baltic republics continued to generate interest and excitement in the Ukraine. In fact, they were held up as models by Ukrainian dissidents during the mass public meetings held in Lvov during the summer of 1988. At a meeting on July 21, the newly released Ukrainian political prisoner Hryhoriy Prykhodko told a crowd about the remarkable degree of national self-assertiveness he had just witnessed during a stopover in Estonia. Another speaker, Bohdan Horyn, acknowledged that people were frequently asking why the sort of things that were happening in Estonia were not happening in Ukraine and, especially, why there was no Ukrainian Popular Front in support of restructuring that would unite all patriotic forces. The reason, he argued, was that the republic was still in the grip of the regressive "Party bureaucratic mafia" headed by Shcherbitsky.[13]

The Ukrainian authorities did indeed do their best to prevent the republic from following the Baltic path. Their entirely negative response to what was happening in the Baltic republics was reflected in the minimal and one-sided coverage of Baltic events provided by the Ukrainian press. Furthermore, the Ukrainian authorities sought to prevent the development of a Baltic-type Ukrainian Popular Front. Unauthorized public meetings in Lvov were broken up by riot police, and numerous dissidents were warned, detained or attacked in the local press. In Kiev, the founders of the Popular Union were not allowed to hold a meeting until the end of September, and then only behind closed doors.[14]

Another indication of the nervousness of the Ukrainian authorities about possible "contagion" from the Baltic republics is the way representa-

---

[12] *Literaturna Ukraina*, July 18, 1988.

[13] This account is based on cassette recordings of the meeting.

[14] Bohdan Nahaylo, "Lvov Authorities Resort to Old Methods in Breaking Up Unauthorized Meetings and Religious Services," *Radio Liberty Research Bulletin*, No. 355, August 13, 1988; Bohdan Nahaylo, "Independent Groups in the Ukraine Under Attack," *Radio Liberty Research Bulletin*, No. 417, September 12, 1988; and Bohdan Nahaylo, "Kiev's Popular Union for the Support of Restructuring Allowed to Meet—Behind Closed Doors," *Radio Liberty Research Bulletin*, No. 468, October 25, 1988.

tives of the Baltic national movements were prevented from meeting with activists in Ukraine. In October, 1988, for example, one of the leading Ukrainian informal patriotic associations—the Lvov-based Tovarystvo Leva (Lion Society)—planned to hold a conference to which it had invited guests from the Baltic Popular Fronts. Not only was the Lion Society denied premises in which to hold the meeting, but the Baltic representatives were intercepted when they arrived in Lvov and sent back.[15]

Ukrainian activists who traveled to the Baltic republics did not face such difficulties. On September 24–25, 1988, Ukrainians were represented at a follow-up meeting in Riga of the Coordinating Committee of the Patriotic Movements of the Peoples of the Soviet Union.[16]

Elements within the Ukrainian Komsomol also displayed enthusiasm for what the Balts were doing. The head of the Lion Society, for instance, a man named Orest Sheyka, was a local Komsomol official. The Lion Society is known to have maintained contacts with activists in the Baltic republics after being prevented from holding its conference in October.

The attitude of the Ukrainian Komsomol's organ, *Molod Ukrainy* (which has a circulation of some 600,000), was especially noteworthy. Whereas the rest of the Ukrainian press remained silent about the crystallization of the Popular Fronts in the Baltic republics, in September and October, 1988, this daily devoted an entire page each to the situations in Latvia, Lithuania and Estonia. The coverage included interviews with leading Lithuanian and Estonian activists as well as a highly favorable report about the inaugural congress of the Estonian Popular Front. The latter was written by a special correspondent who acknowledged that he and his colleagues had been "amazed" by what they had witnessed.[17]

In November, 1988, during the constitutional crisis precipitated by the Gorbachev leadership's announcement of amendments to the Soviet Constitution that would have had the effect of reducing still further the rights of the non-Russian republics, there were conflicting official and unofficial responses in Ukraine. On the one hand, on November 23, the Ukrainian SSR Supreme Soviet condemned the defiant stand taken by the Estonian SSR Supreme Soviet in reaffirming the sovereignty of Estonia.[18] On the other hand, there were both explicit and implicit unofficial statements of support for the position adopted by the Estonians.

---

[15] Documents describing these events were received by the Ukrainian Press service in Paris.

[16] See Bohdan Nahaylo, "Non-Russian National Democratic Movements Hold Another Meeting," *Radio Liberty Research Bulletin*, No. 465, October 10, 1988.

[17] *Molod Ukrainy*, October 20, 1988; for the items on Latvia and Lithuania, see the issues for September 20 and October 6, respectively.

[18] *Radyanska Ukraina*, November 24, 1988.

On November 20, the unofficial Ukrainian Helsinki Union—the major dissident association in the republic, with branches in Kiev, Lvov, Moscow and other cities—sent a statement to the USSR Supreme Soviet objecting to the proposed constitutional amendments on the grounds that they "further increased imperial centralism in all spheres of social life." The group's leaders also addressed a statement to the people of Estonia and the deputies of the Estonian SSR Supreme Soviet deploring the attitude of the Ukrainian SSR Supreme Soviet and assuring the Estonians that "at this responsible time, the national democratic forces of Ukraine are fully on your side."[19]

A day after the Ukrainian SSR Supreme Soviet had come out against the position taken by the Estonians, the Ukrainian literary weekly *Literaturna Ukraina* published a lengthy discussion in which three Ukrainian legal experts voiced more or less the same objections to the proposed changes in the Soviet Constitution as had their Estonian counterparts and emphasized the need finally to begin respecting the proclaimed sovereignty of the Union republics. According to one of the participants, V. A. Vasylenko, a professor of juridical sciences at Kiev State University, the proposed changes went against "the spirit and letter of the decisions of the 19th Party Conference" to "liquidate the consequences of Stalinism" in relations between Moscow and the republics and to "strengthen the democratic principles of our federation by broadening the rights of the Union republics and autonomous units." Even compared with the Stalin constitution of 1936, Vasylenko argued, the proposed amendments were "a step backwards."

His colleague P. F. Martynenko, a candidate of juridical sciences, summarized why the proposed changes were unacceptable from the point of view of the Union republics:

> Such an approach cannot be agreed with in view of the fact that, according to the Soviet Constitution, the Soviet Union and the Union republics are sovereign states. This means that, in realizing their powers, they are obliged *to respect one another's sovereignty* [emphasis in original].

The third legal specialist, V. V. Rudnytskyi, disclosed that he, Vasylenko, Martynenko and V. M. Selivanov, a leading scientific worker at the Ukrainian SSR Academy of Sciences' Institute of State and Law, had submitted an alternative draft of the section in the proposed amendments dealing with "the national-state structure of the Soviet Union."[20]

---

[19] Ukrainian Press Agency, London, press releases, No. 184, December 2, 1988; and No. 185, December 8, 1988.

[20] "Bilshe sotsializmu—bilshe narodovladdya," *Literaturna Ukraina*, November 24, 1988.

The language question was another area in which the Ukrainians were inspired by the Balts' example. At least since the beginning of 1987, nationally minded Ukrainian intellectuals, particularly members of the Ukrainian Writers' Union, had been campaigning for the designation of the Ukrainian language as the state language of the Ukrainian SSR. Initially, the Ukrainian authorities rejected this demand. The successes of the Baltic nations in this regard during 1988 served, however, as a fillip for Ukrainian patriots and placed additional pressure on the Ukrainian authorities to review their attitude. A well-known literary critic, Volodymyr Panchenko, for instance, reminded readers of *Literaturna Ukraina* on November 24 that *Pravda* had recently announced that Lithuanian had been made the state language of the Lithuanian SSR. "Surely an analogous decision is not impossible here in the Ukraine?" he asked.

The campaign in defense of the Ukrainian language had in fact been stepped up and was beginning to bear fruit. In November, two commissions of the Ukrainian SSR Supreme Soviet formally proposed that Ukrainian be made the state language of the Ukrainian SSR. But the Ukrainian literary and cultural intelligentsia were still frustrated by the slow pace of change in Ukraine, and they became more radicalized and outspoken. One of the leading campaigners in defense of the Ukrainian language, the poet Dmytro Pavlychko, stressed in December, 1988, that the language question was an important aspect of the struggle to repair the damage done to the rights of the non-Russian republics by Stalinism and "Brezhnevite great-power policies" and to restore meaning to the sovereignty of the Union republics.[21] The Ukrainian language was eventually recognized as the official state language of Ukraine at the end of October, 1989, though Russian was designated the language of interethnic communication.[22]

In the fall of 1988, members of the literary intelligentsia took the initiative and tried once again to launch a Ukrainian Popular Front in support of restructuring and to promote the idea of concerted action by the republic's cultural unions. The call to create a Ukrainian Popular Front–type movement was made publicly by Pavlychko and the writer Yurii Shcherbak at a mass public meeting on ecological issues in Kiev on November 13. The proposal was enthusiastically received, and the rally turned into a political demonstration. The speakers included representatives from Latvia and Lithuania.[23] An initiative group was formed from among members of the

---

[21] *Literaturna Ukraina*, December 15, 1988.

[22] For the text of the language law, see *Literaturna Ukraina*, November 12, 1989.

[23] Associated Press, November 13, 1988; Ukrainian Press Agency, press release, No. 180, November 19, 1988; and David Marples, "Mass Meeting in Kiev Focuses On Ecological Issues, Political Situation," *The Ukrainian Weekly* (New Jersey), December 4, 1988.

Ukrainian Writers' Union and the Ukrainian SSR Institute of Literature. Despite interference by the authorities, the group proceeded to draw up a draft program. One of the initiators of the new popular movement, the poet Pavlo Movchan, later acknowledged to Radio Liberty: "We had as models those programs with which we were already familiar, the programs of the Estonian Popular Front, of Sajudis and of the Latvian Popular Front."[24]

Meanwhile, calls were also made for a joint meeting of the Ukrainian cultural unions. In November, the head of the Kiev section of the Ukrainian Artists' Union, A. Chebykin, told a plenum of his branch that the need for such a meeting had become apparent.[25] The following month, the first secretary of the board of the Ukrainian Writers' Union, Yurii Mushketyk, also emphasized the need for a joint meeting of the cultural unions to discuss "acute problems in the development of Ukrainian culture."[26] These proposals were apparently blocked, for nothing came of them.

The Party authorities failed to prevent the new Ukrainian popular movement from getting off the ground, for on February 16, 1989, *Literaturna Ukraina* published the draft program of the Popular Movement of Ukraine for Restructuring, or "Rukh" (The Movement). Pressure from the ideological apparatus did succeed, though, in forcing the authors to water down the document and to acknowledge the leading role of the Party. Although Rukh's program did not go as far as those of the Baltic Popular Fronts, by Ukrainian standards it was radical. It addressed a broad range of political, social, cultural and ecological issues and came out for the attainment of "genuine sovereignty" for Ukraine.

Despite the concessions made in the draft program, the Party authorities reacted to its publication as a provocation and launched a major press campaign against Rukh and its founders. This hostile attitude continued into the second half of the year.[27] The Kiev authorities and the press under their control also continued either to ignore the Baltic national movements and the headway they were making or to denounce them. In May, for instance, in true "stagnationist" style, the deputy head of the CPU Central Committee's ideological section, P. Kulyas, wrote in the CPU's organ *Pid praporom leninizmu* that one would have to be "naïve"

[24] Roman Solchanyk, "Beginnings of the Ukrainian Popular Front: An Interview with Pavlo Movchan," RFE/RL *Report on the USSR*, March 3, 1989.

[25] O. Sedyk, "Vbplyvaty na rozvytok mystetstva," *Kultura i zhyttya*, November 20, 1988.

[26] *Literaturna Ukraina*, December 8, 1988.

[27] See Bohdan Nahaylo, "Confrontation over Creation of Ukrainian Popular Front," and "Draft Program of Ukrainian Baltic-Type Popular Movement under Strong Attack," RFE/RL *Report on the USSR*, March 3, 1989.

not to foresee the serious political implications of the "further anti-socialist transformation" of Rukh's draft program—"as had already happened in the case of the programs of the Popular Fronts in the Baltic republics."[28]

The spring, 1989, elections to the new Congress of People's Deputies brought quite a few surprises in Ukraine. Although the majority of the people's deputies elected were conservatives put forward by the Ukrainian Party apparatus, the latter suffered quite a few humiliating defeats, and a number of reformist and nationally minded candidates—including several leaders of Rukh—were elected. They were soon to form their own Ukrainian Republican Deputies' Club and make common cause with democratic candidates from the Baltic and elsewhere; in the summer they united with them in an alliance known as the Interregional Deputies Group. The Kiev writer and deputy Volodymyr Yavorivsky told Radio Liberty's Ukrainian Service in a telephone interview on June 14, 1989, that he and other democratic Ukrainian deputies had, from their very first day in the new congress, gotten on well with the Baltic deputies; they had voted with them against what Moscow historian Yurii Afanasev labeled the "aggressively obedient majority."

Democratic Ukrainian deputies also spoke out at the congress in support of the Baltic plan for economic autonomy, which initially came under heavy attack from the central planners and conservatives. On July 8, the Lvov deputy Rostyslav Bratun defended the Baltic scheme for "sovereignty and republican cost-accounting."[29] Another deputy from Ukraine, Anatolii Saunin from the Donbas, who was not a member of the Ukrainian democratic faction, hailed the scheme for economic autonomy advanced by the Balts as a "revolutionary step in the restructuring of the country's economic mechanism."[30] When the Balts finally won their victory on this score, the Kiev deputy Yurii Shcherbak called it an "historical day," expressed his hope that all the republics would now be able to follow the Balts' economic route and registered his regret that it had not been Ukraine that had initiated the breakthrough.[31]

For Rukh, the Ukrainian Helsinki Union and other Ukrainian informal organizations, the Baltic republics became not only a source of inspiration but of support and practical help. Publications of the Baltic Popular Fronts, such as the Latvian newspaper *Atmoda*, gave sympathetic coverage of the Ukrainian national movement. What is more (although it is hard, for obvious reasons, to document this), it is known that on numerous

---

[28]   *Pid praporom leninizmu*, No. 10 (May, 1989), 49.

[29]   Radio Moscow broadcast, July 8, 1989.

[30]   *Ibid.*, July 26, 1989.

[31]   *Ibid.*, July 27, 1989.

occasions Ukrainian independent organizations circumvented the obstacles and restrictions placed on their activities in Ukraine by printing their materials in the Baltic republics.[32] One Ukrainian opposition group, the Ukrainian People's Democratic League, held its founding congress in Riga on June 24–25, 1989.

The Balts' support set a useful precedent for Rukh, for it afforded the Ukrainian movement with crucial leverage over Ukrainian authorities. When Rukh finally held its founding congress in Kiev on September 8–10, 1989, Reuters reported that

> Rukh leaders said they were given permission for the Congress only after its organizers made clear that if they were refused they would travel to Lithuania, whose reformist party leadership was prepared to let it take place there.[33]

Although Shcherbitsky was replaced at the end of September by Volodymyr Ivashko, the latter showed no signs of being a Ukrainian Brazauskas or Valjas. While paying lip service to restructuring and democratization, the Ukrainian Party and state apparatus continued to defend the status quo. At the end of November, Serhii Konev, a deputy to the Soviet Union Congress of People's Deputies and a deputy leader of Rukh, attacked Ukraine's Party and state apparatchiks in a speech before the Ukrainian Supreme Soviet. Among other things, he said:

> Many of our responsible comrades scowl at the Baltic republics. Naturally! The separatists and nationalists are demanding something special for themselves! But what it is that they are demanding? A guaranteed future for themselves and their children, respect for their own distinct culture and state sovereignty for their republics. On the other hand, how much longer is Ukraine going to go around gagged and under false slogans while surrendering its native land and the future of its nation for squandering by the All-Union bureaucracy?

On August 23, 1989, the Baltic nations marked the 50th anniversary of the Molotov-Ribbentrop Pact with a human chain linking Tallinn, Riga and Vilnius. By this time, Ukrainian activists, too, were openly denouncing the Nazi-Soviet agreement and its consequences for Western Ukraine. At its founding congress in Riga, the Ukrainian People's Democratic League adopted a resolution condemning the "shameful pact" and its "secret

---

[32] *HUL (Informatsinynyi byuletin hromady ukraintsiv Lytvy)*, Vilnius, No. 1, April, 1989.

[33] Reuters, September 9, 1989.

criminal protocol."[34] Leading figures in the Ukrainian Helsinki Union also took this position at a conference on the pact organized in Tallinn at the end of June by the Estonian Academy of Sciences.[35]

On August 21, some 2,000 people took part in a protest meeting in Kiev called by the Ukrainian Helsinki Union and the Ukrainian People's Democratic League. Estonian, Latvian, Belorussian and Moldavian national flags were displayed alongside the blue and yellow Ukrainian one. Oles Shevchenko, the head of the Ukrainian Helsinki Union's Kiev branch, told the crowd: "There cannot be an independent Ukraine without an independent Lithuania, Latvia and Estonia."[36]

On September 17, many tens of thousands of people in Lvov and other Western Ukrainian cities answered a call by the Ukrainian Helsinki Union and other informal groups to mark the 50th anniversary of what they depicted as the replacement of the Polish occupation of Western Ukraine with an even more oppressive Soviet one. Human chains were formed, and in the evening lighted candles were placed in windows.[37]

The Molotov-Ribbentrop Pact and what it represented for Ukraine became even more of an issue as the year wore on. In anticipation of a broader discussion of the pact at the second session of the Congress of People's Deputies, Dmytro Pavlychko, now also a people's deputy, prepared a speech on the Ukrainian aspect of this theme. After not being given the opportunity to deliver it at the congress, Pavlychko published it in *Literaturna Ukraina*. Echoing the Baltic view of the agreement, he dwelt on the tragic impact this "shameful consequence" of Hitler's and Stalin's "imperial policy" had for Western Ukraine: mass deportations, executions, forced collectivization and the "debasement of national dignity." As in the Baltic, Pavlychko viewed the Nazi-Soviet collusion as an affront "to Ukrainian history" and as an act that totally disregarded the "sovereignty" of the Ukrainian people. The lesson, he argued, was that "only the independence of the Soviet republics" could guarantee an "honest" way forward for "our union state."[38]

At the beginning of 1990, Pavlychko also headed a major manifestation of Ukrainian unity and national assertiveness. It was organized by Rukh, together with the Ukrainian Helsinki Union and other movements to mark

[34] Ukrainian Press Agency, press releases, No. 118, August 1, 1989; and No. 142, August 1, 1989.

[35] Ukrainian Press Agency, press release, No. 144, August 2, 1989. For examples of other statements by Ukrainian democrats condemning the Molotov-Ribbentrop Pact, see press release, No. 143, July 30, 1989.

[36] Ukrainian Press Agency, press release, No. 140, August 26, 1989.

[37] Reuters, September 18, 1989.

[38] *Literaturna Ukraina*, January 4, 1990.

the anniversary of the unification on January 22, 1919, of the formerly Russian-ruled Ukraine with the western part of Ukraine (once under Austria-Hungary) in an independent, albeit short-lived, Ukrainian state. Drawing on the impressive Baltic example, it took the form of a human chain stretching from Kiev to Lvov. The manifestation took place on January 21, and was supported by many hundreds of thousands of people. Only a few months earlier, such an action would have been unthinkable. Interestingly, in Kiev, quite a few participants in the human chain are reported to have held Baltic national flags.[39]

There were also signs of Ukrainian support for the Lithuanians when Gorbachev went to Lithuania in the spring of 1990 to attempt to persuade the Lithuanian Communists not to break away from Moscow. During the coverage of his activities in Vilnius on Soviet television's evening newscast, *Vremya*, numerous Ukrainian blue and yellow national flags, presumably carried by local Ukrainian residents, were discernible in the sea of Lithuanian flags.

Confirmation of how closely Ukrainians were watching events in the Baltic was provided on January 12, 1990, when Radio Kiev's external service reported that the "problems of renewing the Soviet federation" raised by Gorbachev in Lithuania had "literally jolted the political activity of the inhabitants of Ukraine." As an example of the growing realization in the republic that "it is important to alter the federation itself and the position of each republic and people," Radio Kiev cited a resolution on the Soviet Union that was passed at a meeting of the Ukrainian Republican Deputies' Club. According to the radio service, the democratic Ukrainian deputies stressed that the "unitary pseudosocialist centralized empire" formed as a result of the "great-power policy of Stalin and his clique" had ended in failure and that one of the fundamental aims of restructuring had to be the "creation of a genuinely voluntary union of sovereign states and peoples who have realized their self-determination."[40] In other words, at the beginning of the 1990s, the representatives of Ukraine's national democratic forces were openly calling for more or less the same thing as their Baltic colleagues.

The 1990s also began with further displays of Baltic support for the Ukrainian national cause. On January 27–28, the Latvian Popular Front sponsored a conference in Jurmala on "Ukrainian Independent Statehood and Ways of Achieving It." The session brought together representatives of various Ukrainian political currents and of Ukrainian societies from as far away as Siberia. The main organizer, Riga Ukrainian activist Oles Tsaruk,

---

[39] See Bohdan Nahaylo, "Human Chain Demonstration in Ukraine: A Triumph for Rukh," RFE/RL *Report on the USSR*, February 2, 1980.

[40] Radio Kiev broadcast, January 12, 1990.

told Radio Liberty's Ukrainian Service that the conference epitomized the "splendid understanding and cooperation" between nationally conscious Ukrainians living in Latvia and the Latvian national movement.[41]

The benevolent attitude of the Baltic national movements toward Ukrainian patriots living in the Baltic republics brought new opportunities for those Ukrainians to organize their own societies and to begin dealing with their cultural needs. Ukrainian societies were formed in Vilnius, Riga, Tallinn and Tartu. Opposed to the interfronts, the members of these societies wholeheartedly supported the Baltic Popular Fronts.[42]

In general, all Ukrainians seeking a real change for the better, democratization and national emancipation have clearly welcomed the headway made by the Balts and drawn inspiration from it. All the same, by the beginning of the 1990s, although there was considerable mutual sympathy and support for one another, cooperation between the Ukrainian and the Baltic national movements was still rather modest compared with the potential possibilities. In a broader sense, however, the Baltic revolution has changed the very terms in which the national question is discussed in the Soviet Union, redirecting the emphasis to the cardinal issues of national self-determination, republican sovereignty and independence. This has had an impact on the Ukrainian Komsomol and even the conservative Ukrainian Party apparatus. Thus, in its appeal to the Ukrainian electorate published on December 3, 1989, the CPU Central Committee seemed to borrow directly from the lexicon of Baltic reformers when it assured the Ukrainian population that it upheld the principles of the "economic independence and the state sovereignty of our republic." For the time being, though, a crucial difference remains: in the Baltic republics, such words have been matched by deeds.

---

[41] Radio Liberty Ukrainian Language Service, Record of Interview (January 28, 1990).

[42] See *The Independent*, April 2, 1990, and Agence France Press, March 21, 1990.

10

The Popular Movement in Belorussia and Baltic Influences

Kathleen Mihalisko

Several years ago, in one of its first forays into *glasnost*, the Belorussian Party and government newspaper *Sovetskaya Belorussiya* carried a report on an unusual event that took place on November 1, 1987: a group of approximately 200 young Belorussians held a public meeting in Minsk's Yanka Kupala Square to demand that the truth be told about Stalin's crimes against the Belorussian people. The meeting, which was intended to mark a revival of the custom of *Dzyady*—the commemoration of the dead on All Souls' Day—also had the aura of a patriotic rally. For this reason, the correspondent who covered the event for *Sovetskaya Belorussiya* felt obliged to warn against the prospect of Belorussian nationalism getting out of hand.[1] But the story goes that when a Minsk official called Moscow to relay information about the rally, the reaction at the other end of the line was, "Belorussians? You must be mistaken. They must have been Jews."

The story of how Moscow reacted to the news may be apocryphal, but it nonetheless illustrates that observers both inside and outside the Soviet Union are accustomed to thinking of Belorussia as a passive and rather sleepy corner of the country. With a few notable exceptions, the dissident movement and *samizdat* industry associated with the Brezhnev era passed Belorussia by, in spite of the republic's encirclement by such hotbeds of dissident political activism as the Baltic states and Ukraine. In addition, Belorussia, with good reason, has come to be regarded as the most russified of the non-Russian republics. It suffices to point out that not only are there no Belorussian-language schools in the urban areas (although classes and

---

[1] *Sovetskaya Belorussiya*, November 17, 1987. See also Bohdan Nahaylo, "Political Demonstration in Minsk Attests to Belorussian National Assertiveness," *Radio Liberty Research*, November 26, 1987.

nursery schools with Belorussian as the language of instruction are now being formed), but, according to a study done by the Belorussian Cultural Foundation, not a single teacher of the Belorussian language for primary and secondary schools has been trained since the end of World War II.[2] In the Brezhnev era, moreover, a contemptuous attitude toward the native language became deeply ingrained in many Belorussians.

With the expansion of *glasnost*, however, Belorussia has been rapidly shedding its reputation for passivity. An early sign of discontent with the situation in the republic came in December, 1986, when 28 cultural figures addressed a letter to Gorbachev concerning nationality policies in Belorussia.[3] Significantly, excerpts from that letter were published in the Tallinn monthly *Vikerkaar*.[4] (As will be seen below, this was not the last time that the Baltic press proved willing to publish material from Belorussia that could not get past the censors at home.) A second letter signed by more than 100 people from many walks of life criticizing Party leader Efrem Sakalau's stand on nationality issues was dispatched to the Communist Party General Secretary in June, 1987.[5]

Today, the fate of native language, culture and national identity have become issues of primary importance in Belorussia no less than elsewhere in the Soviet Union. Yet other forces, much more disturbing and threatening from Moscow's point of view, have come into play in Belorussia and other non-Russian republics as a result of the Baltic states' relentless drive toward self-determination. Indeed, the "Baltic virus" had already infected certain elements of Belorussian society back in the days when people like Estonia's Karl Vaino were still in power. To understand this process, it is necessary to take another look at the individuals who participated in the anti-Stalinist meeting in Minsk on November 1, 1987.

---

[2] *National Language in the Socialist State. A Document on the State of the Byelorussian Language in Soviet Byelorussia* (London: The Association of Byelorussians in Great Britain, 1988). The document was approved in April, 1988, by the Language Commission of the Belorussian chapter of the Soviet Cultural Foundation, but because of censorship it did not appear in the official Belorussian press until one year later. See *Literatura i mastatstva* (No. 21, 1989).

[3] *Letters to Gorbachev: New Documents from Soviet Byelorussia* (London: The Association of Byelorussians in Great Britain, 1987). See also Roman Solchanyk, "A Letter to Gorbachev: Belorussian Intellectuals on the Language Question," *Radio Liberty Research*, April 20, 1987.

[4] Toomas Ilves, "Protest from Belorussian Intellectuals to Gorbachev Published in Estonia," *Radio Free Europe Research*, June 15, 1987.

[5] *Listy do Harbochova*, No. 2 (London: The Association of Byelorussians in Great Britain, 1987).

That meeting was organized by two informal youth associations called "Tuteishyya" and "Talaka." The former, which came into being in the spring of 1987, is composed of young writers and poets who are dedicated to the regeneration of a national literature in the Belorussian tongue. (The name Tuteishyya, which means "The Locals," was taken from the title of a play by Yanka Kupala and evokes Belorussia's long status as a provincial backwater of the Russian empire.) Talaka, on the other hand, is open to youth of all backgrounds and professions who wish to revive the use of the Belorussian language and restore a sense of patriotism, national values and civic-mindedness among their fellow citizens.[6] Not surprisingly, the Talaka association came to provide an essential conduit for the spread of ideas from the Baltic states.

The precursor to Talaka was called "Beloruskaya Maistrounya" (The Belorussian Workshop), a grouping of Minsk university students formed in the winter of 1980–81 that engaged in such seemingly innocuous pastimes as folklore expeditions, theater and language study—first and foremost, the Belorussian language, but also Polish, Lithuanian and Esperanto. (Only in 1989 did one of the original members of Maistrounya reveal that the group had been inspired by the emergence of Poland's Solidarity movement.[7]) The association was forced to disband in 1984, the victim of the authorities' suspiciousness. It is important to bear in mind that the interest demonstrated by Maistrounya in things Polish and Lithuanian was once again manifested when, in the atmosphere of liberalization and greater toleration initiated by Gorbachev, the Talaka Historical-Cultural Association surfaced in 1986. Talaka was then and continues to be headed by several of Maistrounya's original members. The group has proven to be enormously popular with patriotic-minded young Belorussians, spawning numerous chapters outside of Minsk and other informal youth groups with similar goals of national revival. From the outset, Talaka was dependent on its contacts in Lithuania for running its day-to-day affairs; the Lithuanians even provided the expanding organization with an office in Vilnius that has telephones and printing presses. The Lithuanian connection also enabled the Belorussians to follow events in the Baltic states at close hand.

---

[6] Information on the early activities of Talaka and Tuteishyya can be found in "Neformaly—kto vy?" *Neman* (No. 6), 1988, 159–168; and in "Use naperadze," *Maladosts* (No. 4, 1988), 143–156. See also Kathleen Mihalisko, "A Profile of Informal Patriotic Youth Groups in Belorussia," *Radio Liberty Research*, July 4, 1988.

[7] The influence of Solidarity on today's independent youth movement was revealed in a speech to the second congress of Belorussian informal youth groups, held on January 14–15, 1989, in Vilnius. The proceedings of the congress were summarized in *Komjaunimo tiesa* and *Komsomolskaya pravda* (Lithuania), January 20, 1989; and in *Niva* (Bialystok), February 19, 1989.

In December, 1987, some 30 Belorussian groups from all over the republic as well as from Lithuania, Ukraine and the Russian Federation held a joint conference near Minsk. The outcome bore witness to the Baltic leanings of the increasingly influential unofficial youth groups: one of the invited guests from the Komsomol complained that the "informals" placed undue emphasis on Belorussia's historical ties with Poland and Lithuania to the detriment of the unity of the Belorussian, Ukrainian and Russian peoples.[8] However, the youth also pledged to fight for constitutional guarantees for the Belorussian language—an idea that was quite subversive by the standards of 1987.

The advent of the great change, called the "singing revolution," in the spring of 1988 had a profound impact on Belorussia's informal patriotic associations and the cultural intelligentsia. In the summer of that year, as the newly launched Baltic Popular Fronts marched from one victory to the next, the demands put forward by Talaka and its offspring societies grew markedly more radical and defiant. Open meetings were held to lecture fellow Belorussians on the history and significance of the pre-Soviet red-on-white flag and the *Pahonya* coat of arms—symbols dating to the time of the Grand Duchy of Lithuania that official Soviet historians have always portrayed as the trappings of Nazi collaborationists.[9] A new umbrella organization called "The Confederation of Belorussian Youth Associations" was formed in the summer, devising its programmatic document directly from the draft programs of the Baltic Fronts.[10]

Another development of great import, this time originating in Belorussia itself, shook the Belorussian public to its core. In June, 1988, the literary weekly *Literatura i mastatstva* published a devastating article called "Kurapaty—Road of Death," written by archeologist/historian Zyanon Paznyak and a colleague, Yavhen Shmyhaleu. The article detailed the results of an archeological investigation they had done in a wooded recreation area on the outskirts of Minsk.[11] The two men had come across part of an enormous mass grave of Belorussians executed by the NKVD in the 1930s, a grave that at one time had contained possibly as many as 250,000

---

[8] *Chyrvonaya zmena*, January 20, 1988.

[9] *Zvyazda*, August 17, 1988. See also Kathleen Mihalisko, "Talaka Takes up Latest Cause: Restoration of Belorussian National Flag," *Radio Liberty Research*, September 7, 1988.

[10] The programmatic document began to circulate in samizdat in the summer of 1988, was officially adopted by the second congress of Belorussian Youth Associations the following January and was finally published in *Chyrvonaya zmena* in its issues of August 5, 9, 10, 12 and 15, 1989.

[11] Zyanon Paznyak and Yavhen Shmyhaleu, "Kurapaty—Daroha smertsi," *Literatura i mastatstva* (No. 23, 1988).

bodies.[12] Paznyak and Shmyhaleu related the testimony of people who had been living in the villages surrounding the Kurapaty woods during the years of the Great Terror and described the contents of the pits they had opened—shoes, women's slippers, coins minted in the mid-1930s and, most horrifying of all, scores of skeletons. For the first time, the Belorussian public was confronted with a part of its history that had long been denied by Soviet propaganda.

One of the consequences of the Kurapaty revelation (and the subsequent realization that it was just one of many such mass grave sites in Belorussia) was the forging of closer ties between patriotic youth associations like Talaka and an older generation of the nationally minded cultural intelligentsia, led by the celebrated author Vasil Bykau. The alliance helped to lay the foundation for the creation, on October 19, 1988, of an anti-Stalinist society called "Martyrology of Belorussia" and a committee charged with organizing the "Adradzhenne" (Renewal) Belorussian Popular Front for *Perestroika*. Paznyak, Bykau and numerous other leading cultural figures were chosen to head both entities. Soon thereafter, Adradzhenne's organizing committee issued an appeal to the citizens of Belorussia that outlined the Popular Front's platform. It called for the development of Belorussian sovereignty, respect for human rights and national revival. The authors were unable to publish their appeal in the official Belorussian press, so, as it would many times again, Sajudis stepped in, publishing a Lithuanian translation of the appeal in the weekly newspaper *Atgimimas*.[13]

The creation of Adradzhenne was immediately denounced in Belorussian newspapers.[14] But the worst and most violent blow fell on October 30, 1988, when Minsk officials dispatched riot police to disperse an All Souls' Day demonstration by the informal groups and Popular Front sympathizers. Never before had residents of the Belorussian capital seen tear gas, truncheons and water hoses turned on participants in a peaceful demonstration, and, not surprisingly, the brutal action generated much sympathy for the embryonic Popular Front.

---

[12] Zyanon Paznyak, "Shumyats nad mahilai sosny," *Literatura i mastatstva* (No. 37, 1988).

[13] *Atgimimas*, No. 8, 1988.

[14] Five conservative academics signed an article attacking Talaka that was published under the title "Evolyutsia politicheskogo nevezhestva" in *inter alia*, *Sovetskaya Belorussiya*, October 22, 1988, and *Znamya yunosti*, October 23, 1988. Further criticism of Talaka and another informal group, Sovremmenik, appeared in "Pena na volne perestroiki," *Sovetskaya Belorussiya*, October 27, 1988. *Vechernyi Minsk*, the notoriously reactionary Minsk newspaper (which is not available to foreign subscribers), assailed the Popular Front of Belorussia immediately after its first organizational meeting. See "Kak eto grustno," *Sovetskaya Belorussiya*, November 4, 1988.

Using the offices of the Belorussian Writers' Union, Adradzhenne pressed on with a republic-wide membership drive and began to publish, in *samizdat*, several news bulletins in both Belorussian and Russian. Because of the authorities' steadfast refusal to give Adradzhenne or the patriotic youth groups access to the official press, the Front's activists came to rely on *samizdat*, the Baltic press and, to a lesser extent, liberal All-Union publications like *Ogonek* to get information into print. Currently, for example, one of the best regular sources of information about Adradzhenne is the "Belorussian Chronicle" that appears in Latvia's *Atmoda*.

If the official Belorussian press has maintained strict silence over Adradzhenne's activities and goals, it has been much more vocal in casting aspersions on the Balts. As early as November, 1988, the media seized on the propaganda line that Lithuania's Belorussian minority was being harassed.[15] In addition, the Komsomol newspaper *Chyrvonaya zmena*, whose liberal editor was replaced in March, 1989, by a more politically cautious figure,[16] published a commentary that interpreted events in the Baltic and other non-Russian republics as a push by mediocre intellectuals and others left out in the cold by Gorbachev's reforms to obtain prestigious positions at the expense of their nonindigenous colleagues. The daily newspaper *Vechernyi Minsk* has vigorously attacked "emissaries" from the Baltic states who want to stir up trouble in Belorussia.

Hostility toward the Balts is apparent in the statements of the republic's highest authorities. Party leader Efrem Sakalau strongly implied the Baltic Popular Fronts when he lambasted "those who are using [*perestroika*] to set the republics against the center, to set one nation against the other and who, with ill intent, are diverting us from the main tasks."[17] Similarly, it was not by accident that several Belorussian newspapers reprinted the speech given at the Congress of People's Deputies by Yevgeny Yarovoi, a Russian factory director from Tallinn[18] who had condemned the situation in Estonia and expressed support for the reactionary spokesman Gustav Naan.

---

[15]   See, for instance, "Na slovakh i na sprave," *Chyr*, November 16, 1988.

[16]   News of the editor's replacement was relayed in a private communication. In the summer of 1989, however, *Chyrvonaya zmena* abruptly swung back to the left of the political spectrum. The change seems to have been related to the ever-widening split in the Komsomol organization between progressives and Party loyalists over a number of issues, including the Baltic developments.

[17]   There are sufficient grounds to believe that Efrem Sakalau had an important role in the promotion of interfronts and united workers' movements—groups that were widely presumed to be the creatures of Yegor Ligachev. During a visit to the Chernobyl zone in late August, 1989, Ligachev warmly praised the leadership abilities of the Belorussian comrades.

[18]   Yarovoi's speech was published on June 6, 1989, in Belorussian newspapers.

In early June, 1989, *Sovetskaya Belorussiya* took Zyanon Paznyak and the philologist Adam Maldzis to task for publishing material in the Baltic press that could not get past the censors in Belorussia.[19] Paznyak, for instance, was accused of trying to inflame anti-Russian sentiment with statements he made to the Komsomol newspaper *Sovetskaya Molodezh*.[20] All in all, fear among Belorussian authorities of what they themselves have referred to as "the Baltic disease" has made itself known in a number of ways, but that does not seem to have diminished the keen interest taken by Belorussians in events among their northern neighbors.

Historical studies, for example, have been affected. As was the case with the long-defunct Maistrounya, scholars and youth leaders have begun to emphasize Belorussia's ties with Lithuania in a bid to prove that the origins of Belorussian statehood resided in the Grand Duchy. In this connection, it is interesting to observe that numerous young intellectuals nowadays appear to have little use for the ideals of Slavic unity, regarding pan-Slavism and historical notions of unification as the same old pretexts to justify Russian domination and russification.

In their attempts to keep functioning in the politically reactionary environment fostered by the Belorussian leadership, independent activists have come to depend on more than the Balts' much freer press. In January, 1989, the second congress of Belorussian Youth Associations took place in Vilnius with the help of Sajudis, after the Minsk authorities placed too many conditions on the renting of a meeting hall.[21] On June 24 and 25, Vilnius once again provided the venue for the founding congress of the Adradzhenne Popular Front when the presidium of the Belorussian Supreme Soviet proved reluctant to grant permission for the organization to convene in Minsk.[22] Some would argue that the Belorussians were better off meeting in Lithuania in both instances. Not only is freedom of speech that much greater in Vilnius, but at the end of March, new legislation was enforced in Belorussia that effectively outlawed what had become an important part of all such patriotic assemblies—the display of pre-Soviet emblems and flags.[23]

---

[19] *Sovetskaya Belorussiya*, June 7, 1989.

[20] Zyanon Paznyak, "Belorussiya: Vandeya? Ochakov Zimnii?" *Sovetskaya Molodezh*, April 20, 1989.

[21] See footnote 7.

[22] See *inter alia, Chyrvonaya zmena*, June 13, 1989, and *The Guardian*, June 26, 1989.

[23] On March 31, 1989, the presidium of the Belorussian Supreme Soviet (then chaired by Georgii Tarazevich, who has since become head of the Commission on Nationality Policy and Inter-Nationality Relations of the Soviet Union Supreme Soviet's Council of Nationalities) passed a decree tightening up restrictions against the production and display of unregistered symbols. The decree also targeted *samizdat* publishing.

The program adopted by Adradzhenne at its founding congress in Vilnius is closely modeled on the Baltic Fronts' programs, while taking into account specifically Belorussian conditions.[24] On the question of national statehood, the Belorussian program rests its case not only on "the sovereignty of Belorussia and Lithuania as embodied in the Grand Duchy of Lithuania, Rus and Zhamoitskae" and "the formation of the independent Belorussian People's Republic on March 25, 1918," but also on Belorussia's status as a member state of the United Nations, UNESCO and other international organizations. Among the key points contained in Adradzhenne's program are the broadening of democracy and democratic institutions; the expansion of human, civil and labor rights; guarantees for national minorities in Belorussia; freedom of religion and the legalization of the banned Belorussian Catholic Church; the granting of state status to the Belorussian language; the establishment of republican citizenship; and the restructuring of cultural and educational institutions.

Delegates to the founding congress passed ten resolutions, the first of which called on the United Nations to render assistance to victims of the Chernobyl nuclear disaster. The Popular Front also condemned the Belorussian leadership for attempting to stir up interethnic tension and for waging a propaganda war against Adradzhenne, and termed the Communist Party's monopoly of power a violation of the Universal Declaration on Human Rights, to which the Belorussian SSR and the Soviet Union are signatories. Two other resolutions dealt with Belorussian-Lithuanian relations. At the urging of Syarhei Kuznyatsau, leader of "Svitanak," the Belorussian Association in Riga, the congress considered passing a resolution calling for national independence for Belorussia. Though the delegates decided to avoid making such a radical pronouncement, several speakers left little doubt that the prospect of independent statehood appealed to them in view of the failure of *perestroika* to improve the political and economic situation in Belorussia. Paznyak, who since the Kurapaty discovery has come to be regarded as the voice of free Belorussia, was elected as Adradzhenne's chairman.

On July 1, just one week after the congress-in-exile finished its work, Belorussian Popular Front activists were delivered an unexpected surprise—no less an authority than *Pravda* lashed out at the Belorussian authorities for being intolerant and inflexible and for "using outdated methods that could lead to popular discontent."[25] Worst of all, from the

---

[24] For an account of the proceedings and description of the program, see Kathleen Mihalisko, "Belorussian Popular Front Holds Founding Congress in Vilnius," RFE/RL *Report on the USSR*, July 14, 1989, 13–16. Adradzhenne's program is still available only in the *samizdat* press.

[25] *Pravda*, July 1, 1989.

authorities' point of view, the Party daily criticized a speech made by Sakalau to a Belorussian Party plenum for its lack of substance and fresh ideas. After *Pravda's* critique, Belorussia's leaders apparently made a decision to lift the veil of silence over Adradzhenne just a bit, though still not enough to allow even the outspoken literary weekly *Literatura i mastatstva* to publish the Popular Front's programmatic documents. The Belorussian Komsomol, which is as crisis-ridden as its counterparts in other republics, began to seek a dialogue with Talaka and the Popular Front. In August, one of the Komsomol's highest officials offered assurances that the official youth organization would cooperate with Adradzhenne.[26]

Yet even these few encouraging indications were marred by the Belorussian leadership's continued preference for old-fashioned hate campaigns. *Chyrvonaya zmena*, for instance, produced a letter signed by one V. Vlasov from Riga that claimed (falsely) that the Latvians had forced the Svitanak club to close down; therefore, Vlasov wrote, his fellow Belorussians had little choice but to start up an "interbelfront" in order to struggle against the Latvians' "vulgar nationalism."[27] Over the course of the summer, indeed, the interfronts provided much material for the Belorussian press, primarily in the form of interviews with their representatives.[28] In early August, BelTA, the Belorussian press agency, distributed a collective letter from Belorussians living in Lithuania alleging that the "principles of *perestroika* and the ideas of national renewal propagated by Sajudis have now turned into openly nationalist actions that infringe on the rights of the non-Lithuanian population, including Belorussians."[29]

---

[26] See *Znamya yunosti*, September 3, 1989, for a round-table discussion between Belorussian Komsomol secretary Kanstantsin Astrynski and members of the informal youth groups. According to a report from Minsk to Radio Liberty, however, not all of Astrynski's statements were recorded in that issue of *Znamya yunosti*. Among those left out was his assurance that the Belorussian Komsomol (or at least that faction of it headed by Astrynski) was ready to embrace nearly all the goals of Belorussia's independent youth activists. Astrynski also reportedly deplored the statement issued on August 26 by the Communist Party Central Committee on the situation in the Baltic states.

[27] *Chyrvonaya zmena*, July 29, 1989.

[28] Unofficial sources in Minsk have asserted that in the summer of 1989, interfront activists were not only interviewed by local newspapers but were also invited to give lectures at factory meetings.

[29] The letter, which is of dubious authenticity, was published in a number of Belorussian newspapers on August 10–12, 1989. See *Komsomolskaya pravda* (Lithuania), August 29, 1989, for Zyanon Paznyak's assessment of the anti-Baltic campaign in the press.

A crescendo was reached in the August 15 issue of *Sovetskaya Belorussiya*: spread out over pages two and three were an interview with V. Ivanov from Lithuania's interfront "Yedinstvo," a talk with one of the initiators of the collective letter from Lithuania, an account (reprinted from *Sovetskaya Estonia*) of an Intermovement meeting in Tallinn attended by Yevgeny Yarovoi and—in a none-too-subtle pitch to Slavic solidarity—a reprint from *Pravda Ukrainy* concerning a controversy over the 280th anniversary of the Battle of Poltava. (Ukrainian activists had managed to thwart plans by military-patriotic clubs in the RSFSR, Ukraine and Belorussia to celebrate Russia's victory over the Swedes.[30]) The message was clear: the Balts—whether Latvian, Lithuanian or even Swedish—should be generally regarded as the past and present-day adversaries of the Slavic peoples.

Yet this barrage of propaganda, coupled with the Communist Party Central Committee statement of August 26, 1989, condemning events in the Baltic states, did little but demonstrate the bankruptcy of the Party leadership in Minsk and raise questions about the Kremlin's commitment to overhauling the Soviet federation. At the present time, the chances for Belorussia to become a democratic and sovereign nation are linked in the minds of many to future developments in Vilnius, Riga and Tallinn. Moscow has failed to address the present grievances of the Belorussian people—including the nightmare of Chernobyl, the parlous state of the Belorussian language, the horrors of Kurapaty and the continued lack of basic human rights—and hence has lost the trust of a once most trustworthy of Soviet peoples.

---

[30] The original article was published in *Pravda Ukrainy* on July 23, 1989, under the title "Nashe znamya krasnoe, a petlyurovskogo nam ne nado."

PART FIVE

The West

11

Western Press, Public Opinion and Policy: Discussion

Robert Gillette opened the panel by noting that two premises would guide the discussion. The first was that what the Western press wrote about the Baltic really mattered. It affected Western perceptions of Baltic aspirations, history and peoples, and, ultimately, it affected the attitude of Western governments. In the long term, Western perceptions would come to bear on the fate of the Baltic people. The second premise was that there existed a misunderstanding of the Western press on the part of the Baltic popular movements: of its limitations, of reporters' attitudes and of the obstacles they faced to doing straightforward reporting, even under *glasnost*.

The reporters on the panel were asked to present their views as to the strengths and weaknesses of Western reporting as it pertained to the Baltic. The panelists were Andrew Nagorski of *Newsweek* magazine, who had been its Moscow correspondent until he had been expelled in 1982; Scott Shane, who was the current Moscow correspondent of the Baltimore *Sun;* George Urban, a distinguished scholar and former director of Radio Free Europe; and Carl Gustav Stroehm of *Die Welt*, who is a highly regarded correspondent.

Mr. Nagorski began by reviewing the differences between "covering the Baltic" in the past and today. He had first ventured to the Baltic—specifically to Lithuania—with Mr. Gillette in 1981. As often happened, there was an attempt to prevent them from going. Their hotel in Lithuania claimed a telegram had been sent to Moscow informing both reporters that no rooms were available. They ended up spending the night in a private home—which was not supposed to happen. In 1981, it was very common to be denied permission to travel to the Baltic, and if one got there, surveillance was extremely heavy. Correspondents had a choice of two courses to follow. One was to take the official Foreign Ministry trip. This meant getting the official line and little else. The other was for a reporter to go on his own and simply talk to people on the street, to make whatever contact he could make, usually with people who had been in prison or who had relatives in prison. More enterprising reporters followed the latter course.

On revisiting all three Baltic republics in February, 1989, Mr. Nagorski said, he discovered that he could call anyone he wished. Within moments of starting the first interview with the leader of the Estonian Heritage Society, Mr. Nagorski's interlocutor explained how Estonia might consider temporary membership in the Warsaw Pact after independence. There now was a wealth of people who would talk without fear and on the record.

It was as dramatic a change as in Poland. In 1988, Mr. Nagorski related, he had had dinner with Adam Michnik, who had said: "Oh, by the way, after dinner I'm going into hiding for a few days, because there is another roundup going on." The last time he'd been in Poland, in April of 1989, he had again dined with Mr. Michnik, who this time had said: "Oh, I'm sorry, this will have to be a pretty brief meeting, because I have to go and edit my newspaper; its first issue is coming out tomorrow and I'm also running for the Sejm."

There was the same kind of novelty in the Baltic. Its uniqueness in the Soviet Union appeared when you traveled elsewhere. He had made a one-month trip, trying to travel as much as he could, and had found that in Russia's heartland and in Ukraine there still were touches of the old regime in the way reporters were handled. In Lvov, a Ukrainian bishop was prevented from saying mass in a private home where Mr. Nagorski was waiting. The KGB, knowing that Mr. Nagorski was there, simply turned back the bishop at the city's borders. In Vologda, a Russian provincial town, a young man had accosted him, offering information on troop deployment and other "interesting details." The old tactics were not gone.

Overall, the quality of reporting coming out of the Soviet Union had improved because such Baltic conditions prevailed. Formerly, there had been a feeling among some in the Western press that it was not worthwhile to get out of Moscow. He and others had strongly disagreed with this viewpoint, Mr. Nagorski emphasized, and had acted accordingly. Still, the returns then were less than the returns now. And now that the possibilities of wider contacts were greater, people also were doing a better job of taking advantage of them.

Scott Shane said that he had been in Moscow for a year and a half and hoped no one thought the less of him because he had not yet been expelled—but that it was a lot harder to be expelled now than it had been in 1982, and there still was a chance that he would be. The real problem a single reporter in a one-man Moscow bureau faced when covering other republics was that so much was happening in Moscow it was hard to get away, and events outside Moscow often had to be covered using the telephone. As Mr. Nagorski had said, it was somewhat easier to cover stories in the Baltic than in other parts of the Soviet Union, because everyone was willing to talk and all were very helpful. However, it still was difficult, particularly when writing a deadline story. Two sources could be drawn upon. First, there was the Soviet media. They varied greatly: occasionally you got disinformation; usually you got a mixture. You did not know what was right or wrong, what the overall picture was or how it was distorted. Therefore, you went outside official channels—you "worked the phones." Especially on deadline stories, this could be tricky.

Mr. Shane introduced an example: a recent strike in Tallinn. On July 24 or 25, 1989, he had heard that a strike by Russians was taking place. This was an obvious story—you had to write about it. The key question was: how many people were involved; how big an event was it? He had called the Estonian Popular Front, a good place to start, although they were opposed to the strike. The Popular Front representative had downplayed the matter, contending that only some 2,000 people were involved—why was Mr. Shane writing about it? Interfront had provided more detail, named factories on strike and provided the telephone number of the strike committee (which, however, had been busy all night). This was all the information on hand. Soviet television's *Vremya* newscast, as Mr. Shane recalled, had said nothing about the strike; TASS had had little information to offer.

The correspondent found himself in the following situation: little information was available and the deadline was approaching (in Moscow it came at four o'clock in the morning), but, nonetheless, the story had to be written. Hence a compromise became inevitable. You wrote that the strike organizers claimed 60,000 participated but that others claimed there were many fewer; you yourself did not know how many were on strike. And you were not sure that the people you talked to that night knew, because even if one were on the scene, it was not an easy thing to determine. But you were obliged to write these stories on a daily basis, and that probably explained some of the weaknesses that were pointed out in Western reporting.

The other challenge, after the logistical challenge, was a philosophical one, particularly notable when covering the Baltic. Challenging stories were difficult to cover fairly because it was hard to know exactly what approach to take. Two examples could be offered to illustrate this point. In Vilnius, Mr. Shane had by accident struck up a conversation with a Lithuanian poet. Both of the man's parents had been deported. His father subsequently had been executed, his mother had died of illness in Siberia and he himself had returned to Lithuania at the age of six with other orphans. The man was extremely bitter. As a Russian officer walked by, he had shouted, "There goes one of the *okupanti!*" Some ten minutes later, Mr. Shane had talked with a Polish woman, who had said that the Polish-language services in her church had been eliminated. She had gone there all her life, and she was a fourth-generation resident of the city. The woman had burst into tears—she no longer felt at home in her native town.

Both of these people had absolutely legitimate perspectives, and somehow these had to be given to the reader. But it would not be fair to give an "on the one hand, the Estonians—on the other hand, the Russians" presentation since the Russians did have their country and were not in any danger of disappearing. But Western sympathies were, naturally, with the Baltic national movements. Despite accusations or suggestions that the Western reporters' sympathies were with the Russians, in fact they probably had to guard against the opposite—which would be ignoring the other side of the story.

Mr. Shane closed by offering two hypothetical leads that could have applied to the same story on the same day. First: "In a significant step toward independence for Estonia after half a century of rule from Moscow, the republic's parliament yesterday approved an electoral law that strengthens Estonians' control over their homeland." Or: "Despite a massive protest strike that shut down dozens of factories, the Estonian Supreme Soviet yesterday pressed an election law effectively disenfranchising tens of thousands of Russians and other non-Estonian residents in the Baltic republic."

Mr. Nagorski remarked that there were other points to be elaborated. The first point, which was worth emphasizing, was that most journalism in Moscow was done between ten in the evening and four in the morning, when US deadlines took effect. The dictates of the clock imposed a great disadvantage. The majority of reporters—either American or West European—were alone and had to cover all of the Soviet Union on any given day. The *Washington Post* and the *New York Times* had two or three correspondents; most newspapers did not. Moreover, "working the phone" was an unknown concept as recently as three years ago. It had taken off in the past year and become very normal. When he started reporting from Moscow, if you called a provincial official, often you were told he was not there and the telephone would be hung up—very fast. Now even provincial Russian officials would wax eloquent and then say: "Send me a clip." It had been a rapid change.

Part of the problem for reporters when he was in Moscow, Mr. Nagorski explained, was being stopped from leaving Moscow or being harassed if you were allowed to leave. The other part was your own editors. They feared losing contact with their correspondent while he or she traveled around the country. You had to play games with your editors, sometimes leaving without asking and only saying when you would be back. A weekly magazine allowed such disappearances more readily than a daily newspaper. Some correspondents never or rarely traveled outside Moscow.

For instance, some television correspondents in the past would make a trip once a year. A major improvement today was that editors could now find the Baltic states on the map. There was a much higher level of interest in the subject than there had been. In 1981, for instance, stories based on his trip to Lithuania had ended up on the religious page. When he had asked why, Mr. Nagorski said, his editor had replied: "Well, you kept quoting a Catholic priest and it's a predominantly Catholic country."

George Urban said that recent coverage of the Baltic question had been excellent, from Western correspondents in Moscow and elsewhere. When you pieced together American, British, some German and some Swiss press, the result was a thorough knowledge of various aspects of events. It was not that we were not superbly informed nowadays. But being informed was not the same as being prepared for information, and Western public opinion was totally unprepared for what was taking place in the Baltic. Even the digestion of Polish and Hungarian events, for example, demanded much effort, and these two countries had just now arrived within the consciousness of intelligent and informed Western readers. They knew about Poland; they knew about its economic crises: it was a country far away about which they still knew a great deal. But where the inner empire of the Soviets was concerned—that is, the Baltic countries, the Caucasus and other areas—people still were very unknowledgeable. Psychologically, the Baltic problem was not yet on the agenda of Western governments or public opinion.

The reasons for this were many. Baltic history was virtually unknown in Western countries. The interwar years were vaguely recognized as a period when these countries were independent. Their incorporation into the Soviet Union now, of course, was being given its anniversary and quite a bit of publicity. But even among Mr. Urban's friends (many of whom were well-informed), it all was no more than a vague blot on the history board. They did not really know why and how the incorporation was done; even the Ribbentrop-Molotov Pact was for most people something you read about but did not quite comprehend.

This was much to be regretted but was a fact. In part, it was the result of undereducation in most Western countries; in part it was caused by psychological resistance to facing unpleasantness. People felt that matters you could not do or ought not do something about you ought not internalize or assimilate. As long as you did not realize what the issue was or you persuaded yourself that you did not realize what it was, you might not have to act.

There were several other reasons for this psychological unwillingness to face the Baltic problem. It was an unfortunate fact that governments could take on only one problem at a time. The one problem they were now prepared to face in that part of the world was the situation in Poland and

Hungary. These two had been reluctantly taken on board just recently, and Western governments were bending their minds and efforts to doing something about them. But the Baltic countries were not a part of that field of attention, as they rightfully should be.

Why not? One reason was the fear that the disintegration of the Soviet empire would cause a dangerous instability: if the Baltic countries and others were encouraged toward turmoil or secession or even toward giving great trouble to the central government, somehow a chain effect could reach such proportions that the entire security balance in the world might be affected. Linked to this was the feeling that "creeping Gorbachevization" was much to be preferred to sudden, dramatic, unpredictable or cataclysmic upheavals that violence could and most likely would produce. There were subliminal feelings. One, particularly in England, was a feeling that all of this was heading toward another Northern Ireland; Ulster was on the books, indubitably. If this took place in Central Asia or Moldavia, Soviet central power would face an utterly unpredictable situation.

No one should think that former British, French or Dutch imperialists had any sympathy for the Soviet empire. To the extent that Western governments surveyed the situation suspiciously, they did so because of the way the Hapsburgs went down and the Ottoman Empire vanished and the French Empire disintegrated. In Great Britain, there existed a distinctly old-fashioned Tory belief that empires in themselves—unless particularly harmful or threatening—ought to be kept going for the sake of stability and security. Added to this argument was the contention that the Soviet empire was in a state of great enfeeblement that made it much less threatening under Gorbachev than it had been ten years before. Therefore, to keep it going as an irresolute and even pacific state had many advantages. It was like the Austro-Hungarian Empire in its last 30 years or the Ottoman Empire in its last 50: still just holding together but not really threatening anyone, clearly on the retreat. And why not have that sort of enfeeblement rather than violent upheavals to please the national pride of Latvians or Uzbeks or Caucasians?

Mr. Urban was not supporting such statements: he was attempting to convey the attitudes he had perceived among the public and governments in many countries. Moral support, particularly for the Baltic national movements, would be given and was being given, for example in the European Parliament and by certain American senators. But there really was not much more to be said for that side of the picture. Why this situation prevailed was not clear, particularly as far as the United States was concerned. In America, there were several extremely effective lobbies, and the Baltic lobby was one of these. Yet for some reason the Baltic lobby, with all its influence and wealth, had been unable to persuade the United States government and President Bush himself to come out more clearly on the side of the Baltic freedom movements. Such an action could have consider-able effect on the Soviet government, and could prevent some hasty action it might be tempted to exercise.

A European, German and Baltic perspective was offered by Mr. Stroehm, who explained that he was a Baltic German, born in Estonia, who had gone to school there, and that these facts colored his view of present events in the Baltic. Beyond providing him with reminiscences, the pre-war years in the Baltic had also sharpened his insight, a condition he himself perhaps had not been aware of until a few years ago. So he would speak more of the perception in the mind of the commentator than of the here-and-now of reporting.

All Baltic Germans, he said, remembered the independent republics with the greatest admiration. They looked back to Estonia and Latvia through the experiences of the Nazi-Soviet Pact of 1939 (which had up-rooted them from the Baltic), the Third Reich and the aftermath of World War II. In retrospect, independent Estonia was an orderly, prosperous and humane country where minority nationalities possessed rights and a broad cultural autonomy. There were state-supported minority schools, but one also had to learn Estonian in them and to know the language to study in the university. No minority group that had actually lived with such require-ments in the independent Baltic states had found them objectionable or restrictive, so it was quite astonishing to hear that current Russian opposi-tion to language requirements had found resonance in the West. Consider-ing all the national and social problems that had troubled Europe then and still did now, the conclusion had to be made that the Baltic countries had solved and could solve many problems better than the great states.

Mr. Stroehm had returned to Estonia for the first time in 1962. He had been astonished and pleased to see how the historical traditions of the Baltic had been cherished and maintained during the dangerous years under Stalin. These traditions, introduced by the Germans, had developed in the land itself. Under the surface symbols of churches and monuments, there were deep, underlying ties binding the Baltic to the West. The minds of the Baltic peoples were profoundly different from those of other inhabi-tants of the Soviet Union. Yet there was a basic distinction between how a Baltic German would interpret events today and how, for example, an American would. Even Germans, when they looked eastwards, had their outlook shaped by history. One historical attitude, rivalry and conflict with Russia, could not be found any longer. There was the other historical attitude, agreement and collaboration with Russia, an inclination described with mistrust by other Western countries as the "Rapallo outlook." He would not say that "Rapallo" dominated today, if by this term one meant Germany cutting itself away from the West. But there was the feeling that one should not rock the Soviet boat too much. The question of the Baltic states was placed in the context of reaching a settlement with Moscow by "accepting the realities." This attitude could not be identified with any one political party in West Germany: you could hear the same views from Mr. Kohl or Mr. Vogel or Mr. Genscher, and Mr. Franz Josef Strauss had described his friendly meeting with the General Secretary as one of the high points in his political career. This perspective of "realism and settlement" colored the German government's, press's and public's interpretation of the Soviet Union and the Baltic situation.

Mr. Urban said it was important not to leave an impression that the West failed to identify with Baltic aspirations. A full emotional identification was there, much different from what the Uzbeks or the Tatars could receive. Still, he was afraid identification would not be transformed into stronger substance until (if it so came to pass) tanks appeared on the streets of Riga or Tallinn or Vilnius. It happened with Hungary only when people started attacking radio stations and Soviet armor started rolling; it happened with Czechoslovakia and Poland only when trouble came to a head. He had a gloomy estimate to give but one borne out by historical experience: he certainly would not, however, suggest that the Balts should start provoking the Russians.

A member of the audience could not see why there was astonishment over the failure of the Western press, particularly the American, to cover the Baltic states as fully as some of those present would like. Coverage in the major newspapers was absolutely first-rate. As to the more provincial papers, these also failed to cover France, Germany or Latin America adequately. For all that, the Soviet Union had been receiving more attention in the newspapers, provincial press included. Naturally, there were Armenians who wondered why more attention was not given to Nagorno-Karabakh. This space was probably taken up by Baltic stories. Everyone, he said, would be writing on the Baltic states when something very dramatic and very unfortunate happened.

Radio Free Europe's Toomas Ilves thought the press coverage today was quite good, as far as space was concerned. Four or five years before, an American correspondent in Moscow on his two-year tour filed the one obligatory story about Estonia, where he had noticed Tallinn's cobblestoned streets and Gothic spires but little else. If quantity had arrived in terms of column inches, quality still was not entirely present. He recalled a news-agency report that speculated on an "ideological crackdown" in Estonia. The fact of the matter was that the Estonians had managed to oust one of the more Stalinist ideological secretaries they had ever had. Today, there were stories on the Baltic with much detail but little substance. A few days before, for example, the *International Herald Tribune* had featured a front-page story on changes in the Estonian Party's Central Committee bureau; two of its members had been shuffled away. This was quite accurate, but the change was not really significant. Perhaps Baltic stories had to be featured these days. For all that, they possibly had a good educational purpose, at least for the American public. After all, American opinion polls had reported that many Americans happily believed that Nicaragua was a NATO country somewhere north of Denmark. So there might be a lesson in all stories published.

As someone who studied how people perceived the issue of Baltic independence, Mr. Shane had been struck by how differently the Balts, the people in Moscow and the central press thought about the issue.

The Balts were extremely optimistic and, to a degree, unrealistic about the prospects for independence. As to those in Moscow, and he had in mind particularly the politically progressive group, there were great reservations: autonomy would be acceptable, but the line would be drawn at independence. Here, the Moscow inhabitants certainly followed the interpretation given by the central press, which insisted that independence was demanded by a handful of hotheads in Estonia, Latvia and Lithuania. The number of progressively minded people in Moscow who accepted this interpretation had not diminished during the previous year.

The participants in the Baltic movements, however, believed that the Western press should be an integral part—even an extension—of their activities. Recently, in Riga, Mr. Shane had been asked to speak on Western attitudes toward the popular movements in a public meeting—an invitation he had had to decline since he could not present himself as "Western public opinion." The Balts, too, had been conditioned by a long-standing Soviet view of what the press should do—that it states what the correct approach is and what must be done. Therefore, they might expect that declarations of support should be a part of Western reporting—a misconception difficult to overcome.

Mr. Nagorski thought the problem in Western perceptions lay in a certain disbelief factor, an unwillingness to accept, with full seriousness, that not only was the Soviet empire shaky but that it could possibly be falling apart, and that the Baltic movements therefore were not just some strange causes that had no possibility of affecting the course of history. This was an attitude common to the Western public and, Mr. Nagorski thought, frequently encountered among many editors. For people who might not have followed what was happening—apart from reading the headlines and scanning a few paragraphs in stories—it all could become a bewildering blur, a multiplication of events and trends. The best immediate contribution journalists could make was to piece the jumble of events together accurately, and to sort out what was important and what was not.

Mr. Urban said that one way journalists and writers on Baltic events could put good resolves into action was by first resolving that the word "ethnic" should not be used in any stories, articles or editorials that they wrote. It was not "ethnic" causes that the Latvians were fighting for: they were fighting for their national freedom. They were not nationalists in the sense that this word was misused in the West today. They were a nation that had been oppressed and was attempting to regain its freedom. And in that role, they were symbolic representatives of all the peoples in the Soviet Union, Russians included. Mr. Urban emphasized this point because the Russians in the Baltic nations had not yet comprehended this—that the Baltic struggle also meant legitimate liberation. This consciousness of liberation had to be promoted, because the three Baltic nations were, in fact, the advance guard for the liberation of the entire Soviet Union. We were witnessing, he concluded, the greatest economic and political event in recent history, the disintegration of the Soviet Union, and our politicians and statesmen had not yet devoted their minds to this obvious fact, or certainly not sufficiently so. Therefore, one of the tasks the members of the conference might address themselves to in the future was how to make journalists and governments more conscious of this most central issue in the world today.

12

Estonia: A Popular Front Looks to the West

Marju Lauristin

The profound political changes that recently have swept through Estonia have been paralleled by an equally profound alteration in the minds of the Estonian people, in how they conceive the immediate political reality around them. Politics have become meaningful to us Estonians. Until a very few years ago, we were passive, no more than objects of a policy decreed by Moscow. Now we are determined to be active; indeed, we have been quite active. We want to decide upon our own future, its domestic content and its international setting. Among the groups that have been the most energetic in this regard is Estonia's Popular Front, of which I am a member.

It may not be premature to designate one particular segment within the Front's spectrum of efforts as "foreign policy." Moreover, this foreign policy has two parts—an Eastern part, directed toward Moscow, and a Western part, which has in its sights Europe and the United States. Today the Estonian nation (as well as the Latvian and Lithuanian nations) wants to restore its former independent status or to create a new one. All our activities in the field of foreign policy, directed either toward Moscow or toward the West, are grounded in this aim.

Currently, there is considerable debate over what independence actually means. The following questions—among others—have been proposed. Will Estonian liberation be achieved within the context of a transformed Soviet Union where three sovereign Baltic republics would be members of a confederation? Or will the three states be entirely separate, as, for example, Hungary and Finland? These questions, however, cannot really be addressed until an extremely difficult political and legal obstacle to all our plans and all our definitions about the political future of our country is removed. The Soviet Union has not admitted that it militarily occupied the

Baltic states in June, 1940, and that this forceful occupation came as a direct consequence of an agreement between Hitler and Stalin, the Nazi-Soviet Pact of August 23, 1939. The pact, its additional secret protocols, their results and Moscow's persistent denial of these results have profound historical, political and legal implications today.

It is essential that Moscow finally and fully admit the true facts of the matter and put a stop to an artificially contrived and highly unconvincing debate that intends to obscure them. We have heard, for instance, astonishing assertions that the documents of the pact somehow were not signed, yet the entire world knows that the pact with its secret protocols was signed. We ourselves know about it through bitter personal experience. A special parliamentary commission of the All-Union Supreme Soviet in Moscow has agreed, unanimously, that the truth about August, 1939, must be brought to light. Yet Moscow hesitates.

Once the Soviet government admits the fact that Ribbentrop and Molotov signed a secret agreement, several consequences will ensue. In one sense, the admission will be a confession about the past, about Stalinism and about Baltic history. But the admission—once given—will also have political implications, and will carry significant meaning in international law. Therefore, it will have a great bearing on future developments.

If there was a secret agreement in 1939 followed by a military takeover, there was no socialist revolution in the Baltic states in 1940 that created the conditions for them to be voluntarily incorporated into the Soviet Union, as Moscow has insistently claimed. If the historical truth reveals that a secret deal was struck over the Baltic in 1939, then the three countries were annexed illegally and are from the viewpoint of international law occupied territories. Furthermore, according to the principles of international law, the independent Estonian Republic (as well as the independent Latvian and Lithuanian republics), founded in 1918, continues to exist in principle as the sole legitimate bearer of the sovereign will of the Estonian people. In practice, Western states have refused to recognize the incorporation of 1940. Since that year, the United States has had Baltic legations, with diplomatic representatives of the Baltic governments. More facts could be cited, but the point should be clear: Soviet rule is not legitimate.

By now, Western public opinion has registered the fact that the military occupation of the Baltic states in 1940 is a focus for the efforts of all popular movements in these countries, giving them drive and momentum. The very date when Molotov and Ribbentrop signed the agreement, August 23, 1939, arouses great emotions. Recently, the West witnessed an immense demonstration, the human chain across the Baltic—more than proof enough that the Baltic peoples want their independence back, know how and why they lost it and recognize the methods used to frustrate their desires.

Once it could be said publicly that Estonia and the other two Baltic states are illegally annexed territories, countries under foreign, Soviet occupation, something entirely unexpected occurred: the renaissance of a nation, the rebirth of society. This awakening of the Estonian people has brought about a clear realization of how deeply our economy has been damaged, how critically the healthy development of our society has been harmed and how far the educational level of our nation has sunk in its very ability to comprehend and cope with the contemporary demands of modern society.

One of the first goals that the Popular Front has established is to develop and restore the ability of Estonia's society to function on its own in a modern, Western European setting. We remember that in the past, in the years of Estonia's independence between the two world wars, our country had made extraordinary progress in industry, agriculture, commerce, education and culture. Estonia's economic structure was comparable to that of the Scandinavian countries, and our standard of living did not fall much short of theirs. It is not necessary to elaborate on what the Soviet system has done to our economy. Nonetheless, although today our standard of living and the efficiency of our economy have fallen way below those of the Scandinavian countries, they still stand much above those of Ukraine or Central Russia. The years spent within the cramped confines of the Soviet Union not only have imposed a burden under which our quality of life has sadly declined, they also have vitiated our capabilities. We must regain these—and this will be a troublesome and difficult task.

It is to the West that we are looking for examples and assistance, first of all in the economic realm. We are oriented toward understanding practical lessons, exploring how economic systems function in countries that share conditions similar to those in which we find ourselves (but countries that, nonetheless, have been closed to us), such as Hungary, first, then possibly Yugoslavia. From this stage, we shall move toward other countries such as Finland or Sweden, geographically closer to us but economically further removed. All of this of course involves education, in the most straightforward sense. We must comprehend how economic systems work. We must develop informal or nongovernmental contacts with the West for establishing or improving our knowledge in all areas, not only in economics but also in data processing, management, sociology, psychology—that is, in the entire range of modern scientific education and its practical application.

The particular section of the Popular Front that is engaged in economic research and analysis is also very active in attempting to develop direct economic contacts between enterprises and companies in Estonia and their counterparts in the West. We are very fortunate to have received assistance from Western experts, including some from Sweden, and we also have considerable support from the émigré Estonian community. Possibly the most promising but also, of course, the most difficult matter is to get short-term credits for building our economy. Moreover, we want to have our own, convertible, Estonian currency. For these large endeavors, we need connections with and assistance from the West.

The Popular Front understands that the capability of the Estonian nation to function, as an entity, in a modern European economy must be restored and developed as a preparation for complete independence. Without a period of preparation, Estonian society could not function democratically within Europe even if Estonia would be placed suddenly and miraculously within Europe politically. Currently, the Popular Front is working on a plan that will outline real, overall, cohesive economic autonomy. We are not looking for partial solutions.

In the realm of politics, the Baltic nations have real difficulties with practical, everyday decision making. Therefore, representatives from the Popular Fronts have attempted to develop political contacts on a non-governmental level, utilizing contacts with the émigré communities but reaching beyond them. For Estonia's Popular Front, a primary aim is establishing direct relations with political parties in, for example, Sweden, Finland and then, possibly, West Germany.

A further step in this search for areas where relationships can be sought and contacts developed is with international bodies such as the United Nations. Here we may recall the recent appeal by the Baltic Council to the Secretary General of the United Nations. Estonia's Popular Front is presently preparing a proposal, or request, for an appeal to the Human Rights Commission of the United Nations concerning the establishment of a commission of experts to review the situation of human and national rights in Estonia. The proposal will be sent, first, to Estonia's Supreme Soviet.

What is the ultimate purpose of this, or similar, appeals? All of them must be viewed in the context of regaining our political independence, which inevitably is connected with international structures and an awareness of Baltic developments on an international level. Estonia's Popular Front is considering the possibility of a referendum as an exercise of the right of self-determination. We are very much aware that in order to organize and carry out a referendum of this kind we need effective and credible control and verification from international bodies.

An important part of this movement toward the West involves demilitarization. There are Soviet military installations and a large number of Soviet Army units stationed in each one of the three Baltic countries. It should be obvious that we cannot strive toward the goal of political independence and simultaneously turn a blind eye toward the Soviet military presence. We must, however, address this issue as an integral part of demilitarization in Europe; we must posit it in the context of ongoing negotiations for troop reduction and arms limitation. And we would want to see disarmament proceed quite rapidly.

The issue of disarmament offers a good illustration of the Popular Front's approach to foreign policy and the West. Here we have a very specific issue (Soviet military presence in the Baltic states) that is closely linked to our ultimate political goal (independence), which, in turn, is placed in the framework of East-West relations, of disarmament, of European unification, of a new situation arising in Europe. Every issue we have outlined, beginning with obtaining credit from the West and moving through a whole cluster of related economic issues: every single one transforms itself into a political issue as we present it to the West. We are moving toward our goals by passing through a transitory stage in which we no longer are completely in—nor yet completely out of—the Soviet Union. And this movement is taking place in a Europe where a firm and unbridgeable line no longer is drawn across the continent.

Let me review the Baltic situation along the lines of questions I have had to answer when traveling in the West, as I have had occasion to do. One such question is whether the Baltic states will be content with broad local autonomy, a settlement in which we would have jurisdiction over all our domestic affairs, in which we would be states within a state, autonomous but not sovereign or independent. Such a settlement, or offer, from Moscow will not suffice. The Baltic nations already have regained most of their freedoms in domestic affairs—as far as freedom of information and economic self-management are concerned. But this is not enough. We want independence or, as a minimum, the right to determine our own political institutions and economic structures along the lines, say, of the situation enjoyed by the Grand Duchy of Finland under the tsars in the 19th century. This would be the stage of transition, already mentioned, before full independence. According to our polls, 98 percent of Estonians demand to live in their own sovereign state.

Another question often raised in the West is whether Baltic secession would doom the Soviet Union as a unitary state. The implication of this question is that Moscow could agree to Baltic separatism only by firmly averting its eyes from the concern that Baltic secession would cleave the Soviet Union apart. Of course, it would be hard to imagine a situation in which the three Baltic states could break away from the Soviet Union without encouraging other nationalities—Armenians, Georgians, Uzbeks, Kazakhs, Moldavians—by their example. Immediate secession, a policy advocated today in Estonia by the National Independence Party, is not entirely realistic, for the question cannot be detached from the national demands emerging in other constituent republics. In this context, it is useful to envisage the Soviet Union as an empire that contains a hard core and outer layers. The first outer layer to separate are countries such as Poland and Hungary, which, presumably, will end up entirely beyond Soviet control. The next layer would be the three Baltic states, which would occupy a position as countries allied to the Soviet Union but not part of it.

Some voices in the West, voices of political analysts, have said that during the years of the Cold War there was tension between East and West but each side knew what sort of intentions guided the other one and how far one's own side could go. Today, as the turmoil of *glasnost* and *perestroika* has unleashed what the Western analysts envisage to be social unrest and divisive nationalism in Moscow's empire, we hear from them that a strong, unfriendly but predictable Soviet Union was somehow preferable to a Soviet state that is weaker in its present foreign or military policy toward the West but unstable and entirely unpredictable.

This is, I believe, a highly mistaken interpretation of the situation, which conceals within it a threat for the West as much as a threat for victims of possible repressions within the reach of Soviet power—primarily the Baltic states. I am convinced that if the Soviet Union decided to revert to its previous ways, it would not revert to Brezhnevism or the stability and predictability for which some political thinkers in the West yearn. The Soviet political throwback would be to a ruthless dictatorship, possibly a military dictatorship, and certainly one modeled upon Stalin's rule. If this were to take place, there would be two consequences. In the first place, any regime that uses force and violence toward its own people is much more likely to direct violence toward the outside world. In the second place, a new, dictatorial regime in Moscow would increase Soviet military power and upset the present military and diplomatic balance. World stability would not be reestablished but given a shattering blow.

In this way, the result of the calculations made by some people in the West as to what causes stability or instability in the Soviet empire may be entirely different from the one anticipated. Force against the Baltic movements cannot be ruled out completely. If it does take place, the present occupation of the Baltic states would change: the juridical occupation of today would become a brutal, oppressive occupation regime that would reduce the Baltic to the status of a war zone and thereby an area of concern for the entire world. Such a set of events would also demand that the West, at long last, formulate a clear-cut policy toward the Baltic question. For all that, if the Soviet empire, in its final seizure of agony, would use violence against us, the world would be very fortunate if it faced nothing worse than a new Cold War.

I have been told that Western public opinion and all leading Western politicians admire and morally support the revival of Baltic consciousness and the courage the Baltic nations have shown in translating their desires into reforms. I also understand that there is anxiety in the West, divided counsels as to whether a rapid demise of the Soviet empire would be in the

West's interests. I and my friends have had occasion to discuss the possible consequences of the disintegration of the Soviet state with Western journalists and political leaders. We all were of the opinion that a violent breakup of the empire would be undesirable and dangerous. My personal conviction is that a convulsive collapse need not and should not take place. I believe that the current conditions in Russia itself, its political culture and ability to accept democracy, are at a level that will permit a transition from a large empire to a reduced, but democratic, state. To a large extent, such a change would be brought about by the joint impact of Baltic, Ukrainian, Moldavian, Georgian, Armenian and other national aspirations, combined with the opening of Russia to Western media, Western travel, Western communications and Western ideas.

For those of us engaged in the foreign policy of the Popular Front, moving toward the West, working in the West, has been a process of self-education. The insights we have gained into how Western governments perceive Baltic issues and how these perceptions are reflected in their policies have been important and rewarding to us. We need to learn more about the West, of which Estonia was a part until 1940. And the West needs to be better informed and more discerning about Estonia, the Baltic states in general and the entire disintegrating Soviet empire.

13

Soviet Views of the Baltic Emigration: From Reactionaries to Fellow Countrymen

Janis J. Penikis

Throughout its history, the Soviet Union has produced groups of people who have posed a special challenge to the government. Refugees fleeing Soviet rule, legal emigrants and, on rather rare occasions, people exiled from the Soviet Union have been a thorn in the side of the Soviet authorities ever since 1917.

Until the arrival of the *glasnost* era, such people were rarely discussed, and when they were, references nearly always were negative, even denunciatory.[1] Obviously, the motives of people who chose to leave the Soviet

---

[1] Particularly during the last years of Brezhnev's rule and the growing economic difficulties in the Soviet Union, the role of "destructive émigré centers" and "hostile propaganda attacks" from the West was given much attention in Soviet Latvian publications. In June, 1982, an All-Union Conference on National Relations in the Soviet Union was convoked in Riga to analyze resistance to centralization and russification. The main difficulties in Latvia were identified as, first, a "retarded development of understanding Soviet citizenship"; second, Latvia's close proximity to "destructive ideological centers" (a phrase reserved for Radio Free Europe); and, third, the existence of a "violently reactionary anti-Soviet Latvian emigration." On the conference see Augusts Voss, "Darbalauzu internacionalas audzinasanas talakas pastiprinasanas aktualie jautajumi," *Padomju Latvijas Komunists* (August, 1982), 24–39. From 1982 onward, the Communist Party made intensive efforts to "unmask" the Latvian emigration. Some examples of this endeavor: B. Pudels, "Nacionala jautajuma atrisinajums Padomju Savieniba un ta burzuaziskie viltotaji," *Padomju Latvijas Komunists* (November, 1982), 17–22; and Arta Jane, "Nacionalisms imperialisma kalpiba," *Padomju Latvijas Komunists* (December, 1982), 75–78. The Latvian SSR Academy of Sciences was given the task of coordinating all ideological work and the academy's president wrote a study that pur-

Union, let alone those who had to be exiled, were seen at the very least to be slightly suspect; even the legal emigrants who left for nonpolitical reasons could be suspected of some degree of opportunism. To the Soviet authorities, the refugees, exiles and emigrants represent, in some sense, a failure of the Soviet system. To give any unnecessary publicity to such people would be to admit that somehow indoctrination efforts had failed to convince or to educate properly, or that the regime had been deficient in providing economic, social or political conditions satisfactory to all its citizens. That, in turn, might lead others to question some aspect of Soviet life; backsliding and "political immaturity" have always lurked just below the official serenity of universal acceptance of the system.

Even while the Soviet leadership has observed official silence at home over the existence of refugees and emigrants, it has expended considerable resources and energy abroad to keep itself informed of their activities and, paradoxically, to maintain a variety of contacts with them. It is impossible to say with any precision just how large the Soviet effort has been, but the existence of specialized personnel and organizations to maintain contact with a whole range of former refugee and emigrant groups and the apparent size of a publication program directed at them suggest an undertaking involving thousands of people and millions of rubles each year.[2] The difficulties in estimating the magnitude of the Soviet effort were pointed out several years ago in a ground-breaking case study by Tonu Parming, then the chair of Soviet and East European Studies at the US State Department's Foreign Service Institute. Parming noted that, despite its potential value as a further guide to understanding Soviet international behavior, the study of Soviet activities vis-à-vis the émigré communities has received virtually no attention in the West, nor are systematic collec-

---

ported to reveal the genesis of Latvian émigré mentality. See: Vilis Samsons, *Naida un maldu sliksna. Ieskats ekstrema latviesu nacionalistu uzskatu attistiba* (Riga: Avots, 1983).

  [2] The background of this complex story is related in Uldis Germanis, "Padomju taktika pret trimdiniekiem gadu gaita (1945–1975)," *Zinasanai* (Stockholm: Memento, 1986), 43–66. An interesting perspective, from the Soviet side, is provided by Imants Lesinskis, "Cultural Relations or Ethnic Espionage: An Insider's View," *Baltic Forum*, II (Spring, 1985), 1–29. Lesinskis was the president of the presidium of Latvia's Committee for Cultural Contacts with Countrymen Abroad from 1970 to 1976 and, by his own account, a senior KGB officer. In 1978, he requested the right of permanent residence in the United States. Another personal account by an émigré the committee attempted to entangle is given by Atis Lejins, "A Guest of the KGB," *Baltic Forum*, II (Spring, 1985), 30–49.

tions of source materials, such as the voluminous Soviet publications or directories of organizations and personnel engaged in such activities, readily available to Western researchers.[3]

As with so much else, the Gorbachev reforms have had a significant impact on Soviet attitudes toward the exile communities in the West. And as with so much else, the changes are most clearly delineated in the Baltic region. Here, the statements and actions at the official Communist Party and governmental level concerning the Baltic exile communities in the West suggest a stance that could be characterized as a proffer of détente, but not quite of rapprochement. At the unofficial level, however, contacts between the Balts in the homeland and their countrymen in the West have gone through a transformation that would have been unimaginable as recently as mid-1988. Inasmuch as the opportunities for travel and other forms of communication between Baltic nationals and their countrymen abroad still require the explicit or tacit approval of the authorities in Riga, Tallinn and Vilnius (and, presumably, though less often these days, in Moscow), one may surmise that the exponential growth of Baltic East-West contacts is at least tolerated, if not always heartily approved of, by the leaderships of the Baltic Communist parties and governments.

The official Soviet positions on the "émigré problem" have been virtually identical for all three Baltic nationalities in the past, having apparently emanated from the relevant central organs in Moscow. Whether that is still true today is not clear. What is clear, however, is that the main engines driving political and social changes in the Baltic today are the non-Party, nongovernmental Popular Fronts and other "formal" and "informal" organizations. It is also clear that in all three Baltic states, the unofficial groups have reached out to their countrymen in the West, seeking advice, expertise and political and moral support for their respective causes. Such actions on the part of the unofficial groups represent a complete reversal of the traditional positions taken by official Soviet bodies.[4]

[3] Tonu Parming, "The Soviet Union and the Emigree Communities. A Case Study in Active Measures and Disinformation." Paper prepared for Conference on Contemporary Soviet Propaganda and Disinformation, Washington, D.C., June 25 and 26, 1985, 2–3.

[4] Relevant information on the interplay between the emigration and the Baltic countries will be found in Liutas Mockunas, "The Dynamics of Lithuanian Emigré-Homeland Relations," *Baltic Forum*, II (Spring, 1985), 50–59, and Algimantas Gureckas, "The Social and Political Activities of Lithuanian Emigration," *Baltic Forum*, II (Fall, 1985), 16–26. A revealing account of attempts to bypass Soviet controls is told in Mardi Valgamae, "Cinderella Skirmish: A Personal Chronicle," *Baltic Forum*, II (Spring, 1985), 70–87.

The most ambitious exposition of the Soviet view of the World War II–
era Baltic émigrés is a volume entitled *Baltijas reakcionara emigracija sodien*
(*The Baltic Reactionary Emigration Today*).[5] Written by a team of a dozen
authors, most of them associated with the Latvian, Lithuanian and Estonian philosophy and law institutes of the republics' academies of science,
the book was originally published in Russian in 1979. Its 213-page Latvian-
language version appeared in 1982. It purports to describe the origins of the
Baltic emigration and its organizational structure, and to "unmask" the
anti-Soviet functions and "bourgeois falsifications" of the émigrés in the
service of Western imperialism:

> One of the social groups in the imperialist countries—and above all in the
> United States of America, where the opponents of international détente
> are especially active, and where ideological diversionary actions against
> the Soviet Union originate—is the group of reactionary emigrants who have
> left the various socialist states. Among them, a certain place is occupied by
> the emigrant organizations of bourgeois Lithuania, Latvia and Estonia.
>
> The development of this emigration is connected with the defeat of fascist
> Germany in the course of the Second World War and the "Cold War" begun
> by the imperialists against the Soviet Union at the end of the 1940s. Thus, the
> further development and the nature of the activities [of the Baltic emigra-
> tion] were determined by the strategy and tactics of the imperialist states in
> the battle against the countries of the socialist camp, against the growing
> influence of socialism. The leaders of the numerically small emigrant organi-
> zations, who came from the crowd of the German fascist fellow travelers and
> traitors to the interests of their nations, became the servants of the special
> services of the imperialist states.[6]

This excerpt captures the essence of the official Soviet view of the Baltic
exile communities. Their leaders, having escaped just punishment as Nazi
collaborators (and, in some cases, war criminals), have become cogs in the
imperialist anti-Soviet machinery, in which one of their major functions is
to discredit the achievements of the socialist order in their former home-
lands. According to this view, not only the leaders but a majority of the
post-war émigrés are undesirable elements:

> In the main, those escaping to the West were class enemies of the working
> people: former manufacturers, businessmen, large landowners, military

---

[5] V. Steinbergs *et alii*, eds., *Baltijas reakcionara emigracija sodien. Lietuviesu, latviesu un igaunu antikomunistiska emigracija imperialisma kalpiba* (Riga: Zinatne, 1982).
[6] *Ibid.*, 12.

personnel, functionaries of the bourgeois state apparatus, bourgeois cultural workers and also a certain portion of people deceived by anti-Soviet propaganda.[7]

Given this very unpromising human material, the Soviets have lavished an amazing amount of attention and resources on contacts with the Baltic exiles during the last four decades. Each of the three republics, for example, has had (and continues to have) a specialized organization for such contacts, staffed by full-time employees and supported by several hundred more or less volunteer workers drawn from the various creative workers' unions, universities, the Komsomol and the like. In Latvia, the organization known since the 1950s as the Committee for Cultural Contacts with Countrymen Abroad recently changed its name to the Fatherland Committee for Cultural Contacts. The committee's mainstay publication since 1958 has been an eight-page weekly, *Dzimtenes Balss* (*Voice of the Homeland*), with a claimed circulation of 39,000. Although the weekly is theoretically available on a subscription basis, the author's informal surveys over the years of the publication's recipients in the West has not turned up a single person who has actually paid for it.

The Committee for Cultural Contacts has published a whole series of supplements to *Dzimtenes Balss* (*Svesuma Balss, Atbalss, Atzinas un Pardomas* and *Amberland*, which is in English), as well as books, pamphlets and yearbooks. While most of the publications have been of a clearly propagandistic nature, the committee has also endeavored to give credence to the word "cultural" in its name.[8] It has sponsored poetry and prose readings of selected exile authors in Riga (until 1988, usually before restricted, by-invitation-only audiences) and arranged exhibits, concerts and other performances by certain exile artists and musicians. In fact, until 1989, the committee had a near-monopoly on arranging any public appearances in Latvia by exile Latvians. Artists or scholars seeking to make their own arrangements would usually be told by the university or creative workers' union officials that such matters were the province of the committee. In the mid-1970s, the committee also began to offer various cultural and intellectual leaders in Latvia the opportunity to visit Latvian communities in Western Europe and North America. On most such occasions, the individual travelers or groups would be accompanied by a representative of the committee. Also in the 1970s, the committee began offering Latvian films (and later videocassettes) for screening in the West.[9]

---

[7] *Ibid.,* 38.

[8] Germanis, *Zinasanai,* 49–54.

[9] For the committee's own overview of its activities, see *Dzimtene—istenas vertibas mers* (Riga: Avots, 1984), a volume published to commemorate the 20th

As even this cursory review of the committee's activities indicates, a multifaceted and expensive effort has been directed by the Soviet Union toward a group of people, most of whom are officially regarded as bourgeois undesirables.[10] One may speculate that the altruistic motives professed by the committee—to facilitate the émigrés' contacts with the homeland and to help them appreciate the achievements of socialism— are not the only ones to have inspired and justified the magnitude of the undertaking. As Parming has noted, the underlying aim rather has been to try to neutralize the effects of the exiles' political work in the West and to cultivate the sympathies of those in the exile community who are viewed as potentially less anti-Soviet than their compatriots (e.g., the youth).[11]

It is not clear precisely how much the official Soviet attitudes toward the exiles have changed in the Gorbachev era of "new thinking." We do know that, beginning especially in 1988, prominent individual exiles and defectors have been restored to grace in increasing numbers. Thus, the ballerina Natalya Makarova, who defected in 1970, is invited to dance at the Kirov in Leningrad; director Yurii Lyubimov, once stripped of Soviet citizenship, returns to direct a play in Moscow; articles by Aleksandr Solzhenitsyn and Vladimir Voinovich are reprinted in Soviet periodicals; *Izvestia* prints a lengthy article on Joseph Brodsky; and so on.[12] Beyond such individual examples of official tolerance—which of course, may be explained, if one wishes, as adroit appeals to international public opinion— there seem to be indications of a more general policy shift. The Soviet Foreign Ministry is reported to have issued instructions to its consular officers that Soviet citizens living abroad are not to be regarded as "unpatriotic" and that consuls are to "protect the rights of emigrants, prevent discrimination against them and provide them with social and legal assistance."[13] According to one of the authors of the recently published *Principles of Criminal Legislation of the USSR and the Union Republics*, the new republican criminal codes will no longer list "flight abroad or refusal

anniversary of the committee. Although the present committee states that it began its work in 1964, it is a direct continuation of another committee that was founded shortly after World War II. See Germanis, *Zinasanai*, 117–122.

[10] As late as 1988, with *glasnost* and *perestroika* in full gear, the committee continued to reiterate all themes about émigrés of the Brezhnev years. See *Latcij 88* (Riga: Avots, 1988), the committee's yearbook.

[11] Parming, "The Soviet Union and the Emigré Communities."

[12] On these and related cases, see Vera Tolz, "The USSR This Week," RFE/RL *Report on the USSR*, February 3, 1989, and March 17, 1989; and *Radio Liberty Research*, December 14, 1988.

[13] TASS, January 4, 1988.

to return from abroad to the USSR" as a crime, where formerly acts of that kind had been construed as treason.[14]

The shifting, if still somewhat uncertain, Moscow position on the émigré question also has been reflected in the Baltic. A statement by the ideological secretary of the Latvian Communist Party Central Committee, Ivars Kezbers, is illustrative of both the shift and the uncertainty:

> The sovereignty of each Union republic will be strengthened if each will take part more often in the work of [international] nongovernmental organizations. We must more energetically establish nongovernmental personal contacts. The attitude toward our former citizens residing in the West is now changing. We are trying not to depict emigrants and emigrant organizations as enemies, we are trying to find contacts with them and not to dismiss out of hand the possibility of cooperation (we are not speaking here of war criminals and members of the special services). Unfortunately, for the time being there is no common position on resolving these questions.[15]

Kezbers's statement was made at a round-table discussion sponsored by *Kommunist*, the Moscow Communist Party journal, and the three corresponding Baltic Communist Party journals, and attended by representatives of the three republican Central Committees, economists, lawyers and journalists, as well as some leading members of the three Popular Fronts. It was held in Riga, in February, 1989. Whatever the unresolved questions, even the cautiously worded notion of seeking positive contacts and entertaining possible cooperation with the émigrés represents a profound departure from the class-enmity relationship of only a couple of years ago. Abrupt changes in the Communist Party's declaratory policies are, of course, hardly a new Soviet experience, as witness, for example, Lenin's NEP, Stalin's collectivization policy, Khrushchev's destalinization and Gorbachev's own *glasnost* and *perestroika*.

More to the point, however, at least for the current circumstances in the Baltic, is the demonstrated willingness of the republics' Communist Party-*cum*-government leaderships to accept a whole array of hitherto unthinkable contacts between organizations and individuals at home and in the West. For the sake of clarity, it should be noted that we are not referring here to expanded tourism on the part of Balts living in the West, although

---

[14] Julia Wishnevsky, "'Flight Abroad' No Longer Equals Treason," RFE/RL *Report on the USSR*, February 10, 1989.

[15] In *Padomju Latvijas Komunists* (May, 1989), 26. Kezbers changed his views on the émigrés quite rapidly; for an earlier opinion, see I. Kezbers and A. Erglis, "Ignorejot realitates. Par ASV meginajumu atdzivinat 'Baltijas jautajumu,'" *Padomju Latvijas Komunists* (August, 1986), 72–78.

160   *Soviet Views of the Baltic Emigration*

that probably has occurred, too. What is under discussion is the unprecedented series of moves on the part of various Baltic organizations, both official and unofficial, to reach out to the exile communities in the West and the corresponding initiatives and responses of the latter.

The expansion of such contacts has been so sudden and massive that at this point one cannot hope to do more than to outline its general dimensions and give a few examples; a comprehensive survey will have to wait for a more leisurely moment in Baltic affairs. The discussion that follows is based primarily on the author's observations of three meetings between delegations from Latvia and exile Latvians and on personal communications and interviews with Latvian activists, East and West.

The earliest approaches to the question of revising the official depiction of the Latvian exile community appeared in the ninth congress of the Latvian SSR Writers' Union, held in April, 1986. There, the chairman of the union, Janis Peters, urged writers to explore why the Latvian emigrants consisted not only of "fascists of Latvian descent, but also of ditch-diggers and workers, engineers and writers who reject such views." Two other writers, Miervaldis Birze and Andris Vejans, brought up the need to survey the literary contributions of the exile Latvian writers.[16]

While the discussion of the émigré question—at least as reported in the published version of the conference proceedings—was brief to the point of being episodic, the significance of the remarks lay in the fact that an official writers' union had legitimized exile writers, thereby making it possible, by extension, to discuss the entire corpus of the exile cultural complex and its relation to the creative community in Latvia. It bears noting that in 1976, ten years before the Writers' Union conference, Janis Peters, then one of the rising stars in the Latvian literary firmament, had been one of the first of the prominent cultural figures to have accepted an offer from the Committee for Cultural Contacts with Countrymen Abroad of a subsidized tour of the United States, to do readings of his poetry before exile Latvian audiences. At the time, his tour (though not his poetry) received decidedly mixed reactions in the exile community. An equal stir seems to have been created in Latvia by his subsequent lengthy essay in *Literatura un maksla*, the official weekly of the creative unions, detailing in a sensitive and balanced manner his impressions of America and the Latvian exile community.

A second call by the creative unions to legitimize the exile community appeared in June, 1988, in what the *New York Times* called "a defiant proclamation" by Latvia's cultural leaders.[17] The statement, "to regard as self-evident and necessary the radical expansion of cooperation in all areas with [our] countrymen in other republics and abroad," was part of

---

[16] *Vardi . . . Darbi?* (Riga: Avots, 1987), 10–11, 58, 151.
[17] *New York Times*, June 22, 1988.

a broad declaration of national objectives that officially took the form of a resolution by the executive council of the Writers' Union, but was actually debated and adopted with the participation of the leadership of the entire Latvian cultural community—and in the presence of the First Secretary of the Latvian Communist Party.[18] Again, as in 1986, the question of relations with the exile community appeared to be touched upon only in passing, yet interviews with some of the key participants in the writers' plenum indicate that intense and careful preparation of a draft resolution preceded the two-day meeting and that little in its wording was left to chance.

Important as the creative unions' public declarations have been in extending a recognition of sorts to the exile community, they have been rapidly eclipsed in the past few years by a variety of concrete actions to reincorporate the exile artistic and intellectual work into the common national culture. *Literatura un maksla*, for example, has taken the lead in acquainting its readers with samples of exile poetry and prose, interviews with exile cultural figures, reports on exile cultural events and the like. Since mid-1988, nearly all of its weekly issues have contained one or more items drawing on some topic in the exile community. In addition, a young authors' journal, *Avots*, devoted its entire March, 1989, issue to works by exile authors and reports on the exile community.[19] Plays, essays and poetry by exile authors long banned for their ideological heresy (e.g., Andrejs Eglitis, Anslavs Eglitis and Zenta Maurina) also have been reprinted or performed in Latvia. A play by exile author Raimonds Staprans, based on the final days in office (June, 1940) of Karlis Ulmanis, the last president of independent Latvia, has played to sold-out audiences in Riga. The Artists' Union has sponsored exhibits of exile artists' work and a seven-week-long joint workshop and exhibit for ceramic artists from the West and Latvia. In June, 1989, the author had an opportunity to observe a two-day conference at the University of Stockholm that brought together Latvian writers, editors and translators, some 16 from Latvia and 18 from the West. The professional and, by and large, ideological compatibility of the two groups made it apparent that, given an opportunity to continue, the joining of the exile and homeland cultural streams would be a natural process, 45 years of separation notwithstanding.

One must be somewhat less sanguine about the pace and nature of cooperation between homeland and exile community in the realm of

---

[18] *Literatura un maksla*, June 10, 1988.

[19] This monthly journal and its Russian-language counterpart *Rodin* have emerged as the most outspoken and iconoclastic publications in Latvia, and *Rodin* enjoys a readership in the entire Soviet Union. *Avots* was the first to publish Orwell's *Animal Farm*; *Rodin* established a precedent by publishing a cartoon of Lenin as a mouse caught in a mousetrap.

politics and economics. While the contacts in 1989 between various groups in Latvia and exile organizations in the West were breathtaking by the standards of any previous year, the obstacles to the development of further cooperation are considerable as well. Two problems can be readily pointed out. First, from the standpoint of the Soviet central leadership in Moscow and that of the republic Communist Party/government leadership in Riga, much more is directly at stake in the political and economic realms than in the cultural realm. For the past four decades, after all, the major Baltic organizations in the West have based their political credo on the principle of restoring full sovereign independence to the Baltic states— "sovereign" as accepted by international law, not in the current sense of the "sovereign Union republics" of the Soviet Union. If, under the prompting of the exile organizations, the Popular Fronts and similar organizations in the Baltic adopt that credo—as they increasingly appear to be doing, although not necessarily because of exile prompting—the resulting tensions in the Baltic could have incalculable consequences for the Soviet Union. Thus, the only surprising thing about the homeland-exile political contacts is that Moscow and/or republic authorities have tolerated their development to the present level. (The answer to the riddle may well lie in economic considerations—that is, in the hope that political concessions to the Balts will improve the domestic and foreign investment climate to the point where the Baltic republics actually demonstrate the case for *perestroika*.)

The second major obstacle to homeland-exile collaboration in the political and economic spheres is the fact that four decades of separation, official Soviet propaganda and absence of dialogue have produced mutual uncertainties and suspicions concerning each other's political motives, objectives and strategies. The sudden appearance in the Baltic of a wide spectrum of political opinions and of disagreements over objectives and strategies among the various movements and organizations has been genuinely mystifying to many Baltic exiles, whose view of the homeland had become fixed on a simplified image of good nationalists versus a minority of native Soviet collaborators. In turn, the lack of information in the Baltic about the exile community—except through the tendentious presentations of official propaganda—has made the homeland activists uncertain, and sometimes unrealistic, about the exiles' political orientations and resources.

Given these circumstances, a surprisingly intensive development of contacts has taken place in a relatively short period of time. In the Latvian case, at any rate, the lines of communication between Riga and the various Latvian centers in the West have become so numerous that an attempt at a full survey would be tedious and futile. Instead, two brief examples will serve to illustrate the nature of the contacts and their place in Latvian political developments.

The first concerns the human-rights group Helsinki-86, which was established by a handful of workers in Liepaja in the summer of 1986 but was soon crippled by the arrest of its leader, Linards Grantins. The group was revived following the release from prison, in early 1987, of a half-dozen political prisoners. Several of its letters and appeals (addressed to, e.g., Pope John Paul II, the United Nations and Mikhail Gorbachev) were received by the information bureau of the World Federation of Free Latvians (WFFL). Released by the latter to the Western media, the Helsinki-86 communications began to attract some attention in the West and, more importantly, in Latvia, where news of the group and its messages were received mainly through Western radio broadcasts, primarily those of Radio Free Europe.[20] In June, 1987, the group made a major announcement: it stated that on June 14 its members would lay flowers at the Monument of Liberty in Riga to commemorate the victims of Stalin's mass deportations of June, 1941, and invited others to join them. Several thousand people responded, thus setting a precedent for public demonstrations that have now become an almost commonplace phenomenon in the Baltic.[21] One must underscore the crucial role of the exile organization (WFFL) and the Western media in these developments; without them, the messages of the small Helsinki-86 group would have taken far longer to build a mass audience in Latvia.

The second example involves the efforts of several of the major non-Party Latvian groups to establish ties with the exile community. The largest of these, the Popular Front of Latvia (founded in October, 1988; current membership 250,000), sought such contacts from its very inception. Prior to the founding congress, the Front's organizing committee voted (not without some controversy, and by a narrow majority) to invite several representatives of major Latvian exile organizations to attend the congress. Some of those invited agreed to attend, but were denied Soviet entry visas.[22] Since then, the Popular Front has followed two main avenues of contact: one runs to the recently organized Popular Front support groups in the West (primarily in the US, Canada and Sweden), the other to the established major exile organizations (the WFFL, the American Latvian Association, the Latvian National Association in Canada, etc.). Thus, in March, 1989, three leaders of the Popular Front attended a meeting of the Stockholm support

---

[20] On the role of Helsinki-86, see Juris Dreifelds, "Latvian National Rebirth," *Problems of Communism* (July–August, 1989), 81–83; and Dzintra Bungs, "One-and-a-Half Years of Helsinki 86," *Radio Free Europe Research*, February 16, 1988.

[21] Videocassette recordings of the demonstration are available in the West. These were made and distributed by members of Helsinki-86 and other groups emerging in Latvia.

[22] As reported to the author.

group; in April, a delegation of 15 Popular Front representatives met with some 50 support-group activists from Canada and the United States.

The most extensive discussions to date between the exile and homeland representatives took place in May, 1989, at a seminar held at Abrene, the Latvian cultural center in France. Organized jointly by the governing board of Abrene, the Popular Front and the board of the WFFL, the five-day seminar was attended by leaders of the above-named organizations as well as a leader of the Latvian National Independence Movement, the founder of the Latvian Rebirth Party and some 30 academics, journalists and businessmen from the West. Three separate working groups—for political, cultural/educational and economic affairs—discussed the widest array of topics yet to be taken up jointly by exile and home Latvians.[23]

As might be predicted, the most concrete proposals and resolutions were produced by the cultural/educational affairs working group. While the analyses and resolutions of the economic group were equally specific, they were clearly tinged with skepticism as to the feasibility and effectiveness of joint economic undertakings in the absence of radical changes in the Soviet economic system. The political group produced three basically declaratory resolutions (on the Molotov-Ribbentrop Pact, the ecological situation in Latvia and the continuation of the exchange of information between major organizations in exile and in Latvia). Perhaps most importantly, the political group established a more realistic appreciation of the complexity and variety of the political opinions and circumstances that characterize both Latvia and the exile community. One may speculate that, had the meeting taken place in September rather than May, 1989, the position of the Popular Front would have moved considerably closer to that of the exile WFFL on a number of topics.

In view of the fact that, less than two years ago, the only permissible characterization of the exile community was "reactionary emigration," one is tempted to use lofty phrases, such as "historic change," to describe the uncomplicated notion of fellow Latvians discussing issues of common interest. But whatever phrase one uses, it is clear that in a very short time things have moved a long way.

---

[23] See Dzintra Bungs, "Latvian Exile Leaders Meet in France with Representatives of People's Front of Latvia," *Radio Free Europe Research*, May 31, 1989. The author chaired the political group at the Abrene seminar.

About the Authors

Kestutis Girnius is Director of the Lithuanian Service, Radio Free Europe. He has published articles on philosophy, history and current Lithuanian affairs and has taught at Roosevelt University in Chicago. His book *Partizanu Kovos Lietuvoje* (Chicago, 1987) was published in Lithuania in 1990.

Paul B. Henze has conducted research for the RAND Corporation in Washington, D.C., since 1982. He spent 30 years working for the US government and was on the staff of Radio Free Europe in the 1950s. A longtime student of ethnic issues in Eastern Europe and the USSR, his many publications include *The Plot to Kill the Pope* (New York, 1984).

Toomas Hendrik Ilves is Director of the Estonian Service, Radio Free Europe. He was Lecturer in Estonian Literature and Linguistics at Simon Fraser University in Vancouver and has written numerous articles on Baltic and Estonian affairs. Mr. Ilves was awarded the annual prize by the Cultural Foundation of the Republic of Estonia in 1989 for significant contributions to Estonian political and intellectual life.

Marju Lauristin, who previously chaired the Department of Journalism at the University of Tartu, is one of the founders and leaders of Estonia's Popular Front. She is Deputy Chairman of Estonia's Supreme Council, the leader of Estonia's Social Democratic Party and a deputy to the Supreme Soviet of the USSR.

Kathleen Mihalisko is a senior analyst at Radio Liberty. Formerly a specialist on nationality affairs at Soviet Area Audience and Opinion Research (SAAOR) in Paris, she is an expert in Ukrainian and Belorussian affairs who is currently working on a book tentatively entitled *Belorussia and Chernobyl*.

Bohdan Nahaylo is Director of the Ukrainian Service, Radio Liberty. He has written many articles and reviews for the London *Spectator*, *The Times*, the *Wall Street Journal*, *The Guardian*, *New Statesman* and *Encounter*. His latest publication is *Soviet Disunion: A History of the Nationalities Problem in the USSR* (London, 1990).

Janis J. Penikis is an Associate Professor of Political Science at Indiana University, South Bend. His articles on politics have appeared in, among other journals, the Latvian Popular Front's *Atmoda*. He was chairman of the political group at the meeting between Latvian popular movements and Western organizations in Abrene, France, in May 1989.

Andris Trapans, a specialist in Soviet territorial management and military organization, holds the appointment of Professor of International Studies, American Graduate School of International Management, Phoenix, Arizona. A former RAND Corporation consultant, he is the author of several studies of Soviet military logistics, including *Soviet Military Power in the Baltic Area* (Stockholm, 1986).

Jan Arveds Trapans taught history at California state universities and subsequently worked for the US Department of Defense. He served as Director of the Latvian Service, Radio Free Europe, and is now Assistant to the Director, Radio Free Europe Research. His publications include studies on Baltic affairs and history, the latest being *Impatient for Freedom? The Baltic Struggle for Independence* (London, 1990).

V. Stanley Vardys is a Professor of Political Science at the University of Oklahoma and an acknowledged authority on Lithuania. His articles are found in leading journals on Soviet affairs, and his books include *Lithuania under the Soviets* (New York, 1965) and *The Catholic Church, Dissent and Nationality in Soviet Lithuania* (New York, 1978).